BE HEARD NOW!
How to Compel Rapt Attention Every Time You Speak

by Lee Glickstein
with Carol Costello

To Barbara:
Keep
speaking out!

La Glick
2/28/97

Leeway Press

Be Heard Now!
How to Compel Rapt Attention Every Time You Speak

by Lee Glickstein
with Carol Costello

Published by:
Leeway Press
450 Taraval Street, #218
San Francisco, CA 94116

Interior design: Marisa Carder

Copyright © 1996 by Lee Glickstein
First printing 1996
Printed and bound in the United States of America

ISBN 0-9653322-3-3: $16.50 softcover

Contents

Chapter 4

Healing the Inner Speaker 37

Chapter 5

Being Yourself:
The Key to Compelling Rapt Attention 47

Chapter 6

Listening with the Third Ear 63

Chapter 7

Connection is Everything 79

Chapter 8

Vibrant Vulnerability:
The Real Charisma

Chapter 9

From Agony to Ecstasy:
Moving through Stage Fright into Grace

Chapter 10

Creating Support in Any Audience **119**

Chapter 11

The Laughing Spirit: Healthy Humor............**127**

Chapter 12

Transformational Speaking in Business **137**

Chapter 13

Growing into Ourselves: Speaking as Transformation 149

Chapter 14

So You're Going to Give a Talk 159

Chapter 15

The Perfect Opening 169

Chapter 16

How to Structure a
Talk that Gets Results 181

Chapter 17

Your Speaking Circle 191

Order Form

Chapter 1

Transformational Speaking: Genuine, Natural Power

Transform: to change essentially (Webster's).
Transformational Speaking: Living out loud in a way that opens up the possibility of essential change in both the listener and the speaker.

Picture this:

Tonight you are speaking to 150 people. Instead of being paralyzed with fear, anxious or uncertain about the outcome, or compulsively over-preparing and rehearsing every word of your talk, you are looking forward to the evening.

You know from past successes that you can look into the eyes of people in your audience and enjoy rich, intimate, natural connections with them. Your ideas flow effortlessly and spontaneously as you receive the support your listeners send you. They hear and embrace your message because you are at home with yourself, speaking from your authentic relationship with them, and passionately engaged with what you say.

You know your truth and express it in your own unique voice. At the end of the evening, you feel uplifted and the audience is inspired—both by you and by your message.

The simple, elegant solution

A fantasy? No longer. This is the essence of Transformational Speaking—a new way to communicate based on relaxed, natural, authentic human connections, and on accessing your genuine passion. Transformational Speaking gives business leaders and professional speakers access to powerful new levels of connection with their audiences, and offers a way out of the agonizing fear that the rest of us often suffer around speaking in public.

Transformational Speaking lets us compel *rapt* attention *every* time we speak. Even inexperienced speakers with severe stage fright can gain heartfelt support and immediate trust—in board rooms or sales presentations, classrooms or community meetings, around water coolers or coffee tables, in corporate trainings or crisis management, while giving a toast at a wedding or a keynote to 10,000 people.

If you haven't done much speaking in public, you may even have an advantage, because you haven't learned bad habits.

Regardless of your style or level of experience, Transformational Speaking will help you build better business, develop stronger relationships, and be more comfortable and effective in front of groups. If you want people to stop and listen when you speak, understand what you say, and hear your message on a deeper level—even under difficult circumstances—then this book is for you.

The best part is that you can learn and practice Transformational Speaking at no cost, in your own living room or conference room, through the simple, elegant, 100% effective process of Speaking Circles. Thousands of people have moved from agony to ecstasy in front of groups in weeks, sometimes in minutes, in these Circles.

I developed the Speaking Circle process because I grew up "charisma-impaired" and had the world's worst stage fright.

From charisma-impaired to vibrantly vulnerable

My first public talk was a disaster. It was my Bar Mitzvah speech. Bar Mitzvah is the ceremony at which a Jewish boy comes of age— but at 13, puberty for me was still just a rumor. I uttered the traditional opening line, spoken by Jewish boys throughout the ages, in a squeaky soprano: "Today I am a man."

It brought down the house, and I was so embarrassed that I didn't speak again in public for 25 years.

By that time I had moved to California and gotten involved in the human potential movement. It was 1974 and we were all exploring our inner selves. I was also exploring stand-up comedy and public speaking, as a way of dealing with my excruciating shyness. It worked: I learned to be shy in front of groups. I transformed my hidden insecurity into radiant self-doubt. Clearly, there was more to learn.

What set me apart from other aspiring speakers was being constitutionally incapable of covering up my nervousness and insecurities with technique or posturing. That apparent liability gave me the key to everything I know about public presentation. I was always experimenting with processes that would help me as well as my clients—and the day I stumbled on the idea of Speaking Circles, I knew I could be free.

I asked myself what would happen if I *didn't* try to cover up my discomfort, or to pretend that I didn't feel tongue-tied when I did, or to talk faster and faster to avoid the silences, or to memorize every word I was going to say for fear of drawing a blank.

Instead, what if we got a few willing people together, and each of us took a turn standing in front of the group, being wherever we were in that moment? We could do whatever we wanted for 5 minutes—talk, sing, recite poetry, or just stand in silence. We didn't have to cover up our nervousness; it was okay to be nervous, or sad, or silent, or joyful, or elated, or outrageous. And no matter how we were or what we did, the others would give us their full attention and support.

Our only ground rules would be to explore staying connected with people in the audience and *accepting the unconditional support and positive regard of the group.* When we were finished, everyone would give *positive feedback only* about what they had felt when we were in front of the room.

We would bask in a completely safe environment, in that rare condition of being fully seen and heard by other people, and given unconditional support and positive attention. Our only job would be to explore how it felt to receive that much attention and acknowledgment, and to let in as much of it as we could.

It sounded almost too good to be true, so I put together some groups and tried it out.

The Speaking Circles start to turn

At first, some people resisted all the positive attention and support. They complained that being supported no matter what we did and hearing only what people liked about our presentation "wasn't fair," or "wasn't real." We decided that, in order to see whether or not Speaking Circles worked, we would have to put aside that resistance and try it anyway.

The results were astonishing. People blossomed in miraculous ways when they felt fully seen and heard, and when they were given positive feedback for being exactly the way they were. Again and again, we saw that a few minutes of focused support could dissolve a lifetime of holding back with groups, and that those who were already good at receiving support could become even more comfortable with themselves, and therefore more magnetic, more charismatic.

Those who had been nearly paralyzed with stage fright began to relax into a lovely, confident presence. People who had adopted "stagy" or "stylish" personas became genuine and vulnerable. People who had never felt that anything they said would be valued began to find their influential voices. Some people developed the fine art of simply being connected with the group in silence, from their heart and soul, the whole time they were up in front. Professional speakers and entertainers reached new heights of connection and a new joy and wonder in their presentation.

We learned to accept and hear one another in ways that were new to most of us, and deeper than we had experienced before—with the result that speakers told more of their truth. Everyone began finding new places within themselves that were wise, tender, funny, powerful, and peaceful. Even I was able to move from charisma-impaired to vibrantly vulnerable.

It was a completely uplifting and enriching experience that produced startling breakthroughs.

Getting real, and making things happen

It seemed like magic. We had stumbled onto a way for anyone to be charismatic, because it turned out that the most compelling thing any of us could do in front of the group was to be real—to be authentically, genuinely ourselves. That was the thing that inspired trust, and attracted people like a magnet.

Transformational Speaking developed out of these Circles. This new paradigm involves being exactly the person we are in that moment, receiving the group's support, returning over and over to a heart-and-soul connection with individuals in the audience, and listening not just to the words, but to people's essence.

People from business, academia, medicine, psychology, the healing and performing arts, government, and many other fields found that Speaking Circles both enhanced their work and became rich, rapid vehicles for personal growth. They enjoyed speaking more, they were infinitely more effective, and their communication in all areas of life improved.

A growing community of Transformational Speakers has come out of the 2,000 Speaking Circles we've done to date. Today's Circles have evolved since the early days and now include the use of videotape (Chapter 3 contains a complete description), but the fundamentals remain the same.

This book is about what we discovered, how you can make public speaking work for you, and how to set up your own Speaking Circle and become part of this growing community.

The four great truths

In Circles, we discovered four great truths about public speaking, and probably about all successful communication.

1. The most compelling thing we can do is to be real—to be authentically, genuinely ourselves—and no one can do that as well as we can.

Everyone has a story to tell, a unique message to deliver, and a special voice in which to express it. These stories, messages, and voices emerge from our deepest essence, which can speak just as strongly and clearly with silence as it can with words.

In fact, that presence speaks more loudly than anything we say. If we are at ease with ourselves, people know it and can relax with us. The more comfortable we are, the more eloquent and compelling we become. Transformational Speakers share with their audiences a relaxed, natural, and powerful presence that touches and inspires people.

We don't use formal "styles" or "public speaking techniques" because they tend to mask our authentic selves and are not particularly compelling. There is no technique like "no technique."

2. This deep, powerful essence and relaxed self-expression emerge naturally when we are fully seen and heard in a safe, supportive environment.

When we can be completely ourselves—free from any fear of criticism, rejection, or reprisal—our most authentic selves emerge naturally.

As this essence is nurtured over time with positive feedback that acknowledges our creative spirit, the layers of defenses fall away. When we feel that people see us clearly, listen to what we say, and support us without any limitations, we relax into a whole new level of self-acceptance and self-expression.

And the more we are *ourselves*, the more the audience can be *themselves*, which makes the room even safer, which lets us be more ourselves, and so on into a powerful upward spiral.

3. *Connection is everything.*

Transformational Speaking means letting our audience see *us*, and also *seeing them*, as individual human beings with essences as beautiful and powerful as our own. This connection means that, even as we speak, we are "listening" to our audience, and returning again and again to our common humanity and heart-and-soul connection.

The key to instant rapport, and maintaining this connection, is making others feel fully seen and heard in our presence. When we listen to others, they listen to us. When we honor people with our full attention and regard, they listen to what we say, whether we are speaking to one person or 10,000 people.

4. *The key to connecting with any audience is not knowing how to give to them, but knowing how to receive support from them.*

It's not what we put out, it's what we allow our audience to give, that determines our relationship with them.

These four elements of great public speaking—being ourselves, creating a safe environment, connecting with the audience, and receiving support—all work together and strengthen one another. When we do any one of them, the other three are enhanced. The more we are ourselves, the safer it gets, the greater the connection, and the easier it is to receive support.

What everybody wants, and how to get it

As we start to live and speak within these four basic truths, we begin an exhilarating and almost electric relationship with the audience.

We're all getting what we want more than anything else in life— to be ourselves; to be seen, heard, and accepted; and to be supported by and connected with other people. We want that in our personal relationships, we want it in business, we want it in our families, communities, and churches—and we want it both as audience members and as speakers.

That kind of relationship sounds simple, but it isn't always easy. Many of us have spent years learning how *not* to be ourselves,

especially in front of groups, and we have not always been supported in life. Fear can keep us from being real, and defenses can
keep us from receiving support and connecting with one another.

Speaking Circles are the perfect way to practice getting beyond
these fears. We have, perhaps for the first time ever, a place in
which to speak our truth that is completely safe. We will not be
ridiculed, criticized, or interrupted. As we learn to relax and speak
spontaneously, from our own natural authority and wisdom, we
begin to see how we were actually trained to feel tense, and to
hold ourselves back in front of groups.

With practice, we learn to stand in our own light without defenses, posturing, or technique, and to reach out and take in people's support. We connect with audiences in ways we never thought
possible. That lifts us into a whole new dimension of communication—in front of a room, in business, and in our personal relationships.

The ten great benefits of Transformational Speaking

Transformational Speaking is a dynamic process of self-realization and human connection, a powerful tool that each of us can use in our own unique way to understand ourselves, live in the light, improve our performance in the world, and deepen our relationships both with loved ones and with people we've just met.

These are some of the general benefits people have shared.

1. Confidence.

We learn how to move through fears easily and quickly, and become more at ease with ourselves, others, and groups. Even if we are nervous, we don't panic. We know how to relax into that peaceful, powerful, compelling place within where we find our "super natural" presence.

2. Authenticity.

We become more natural and real, and open into a genuine, heartfelt connection with our audience. As we discover more of ourselves, we can express deeper levels of our message—both in business and in personal relationships.

3. Spontaneity.

"Thinking on our feet" becomes second nature. A natural humor starts to emerge that relaxes listeners and makes them more receptive. We learn to defuse the critical inner voices, and move from stage fright and compulsive over-preparation to relaxed spontaneity.

4. Clarity.

We speak simply, clearly, and from the heart. Because we are calm and clear, we influence our listeners in a natural way so they can commit to action without resistance.

5. Self-expression.

As we open to the dance of giving and receiving, we naturally become more self-expressive. We access deeper levels of our thoughts and feelings, and attract greater love, health, and financial well-being.

6. Instant rapport.

We connect with people on a human level and honor their essence, and so they want us to succeed.

7. Better listening.

We learn to listen to people, even *while* we are speaking. This carries over into all aspects of our lives, enriching both business and personal relationships. We also start listening to *ourselves* in deeper, more supportive ways—and discovering more of our own truth.

8. Being heard.

When we listen to people and let them support us, they listen to *us*.

9. Charisma.

We learn to find and honor the unique, vibrant, naturally charismatic essence within us that builds trust, attracts people, and lets us speak to groups as naturally as we would to friends over coffee. That's an irresistible force—whether it's done one-to-one or in a huge auditorium.

10. Personal growth.

We develop higher self-esteem, enjoy better relationships, become more productive, and find deeper appreciation of ourselves and others.

A new way to do business

It's personally rewarding to grow and to communicate more effectively, but business leaders are discovering that the skills we learn in Transformational Speaking also affect the bottom line. Communications experts say that nothing is as compelling as authenticity, and that people who can stand before others in a genuine way, being themselves in all their glory and vulnerability, can get more done and produce better results. Simply stated, Transformational Speaking skills get us more than a soul connection with other human beings; they make us more successful.

"Transformational Speaking is on the cutting edge of what's going on in this country in business," says Doug Krug, co-author of *Enlightened Leadership: Getting to the Heart of Change* (Simon and Schuster, 1994), and an internationally recognized trainer of corporate leaders.

It's clear that what we've been doing just isn't working. We've been trying to deal with the surface stuff, not the real issues, which are people. People want to get real and authentic, and business leaders are beginning to see that they have to get real with their potential customers and clients—and with their employees.

People want to work with you when you can look them in the eye and connect with them on a deep level. They recognize slickness, and they don't trust it. They want to be cared for, treated fairly, dealt with honestly, and given a chance to express themselves and be at their best. They want leaders in whom they have faith, and who have the "soft skills" of Transformational Speaking—support, listening, connection, and authenticity.

Futurist and professional speaker Chuck Moyer adds, "The key to balance and success in business and relationship in the 21st century will be a keen awareness and attention to the basic human of human beings to be fully seen and fully heard *exactly as we are.*"

Until recently, we might not have used these terms to describe successful business relationships. Today, these values are on the cutting edge of American corporations.

Who are the Transformational Speakers?

People of all ages, economic circumstances, walks of life, and outlooks find their way into Speaking Circles.

Most of us want to know and express ourselves better, and to communicate more effectively with other human beings. And many of us are terrified of public speaking! Studies show that speaking in public is the #1 fear among Americans, outranking the fear of death. In the 8 years I've coached public speaking, I have heard this fear expressed many ways.

- "I'm fine one-to-one, with colleagues I see every day or even people from out of town. But put me in front of three or more people, and I freeze up. It's as if somebody reached in and cauterized my brain cells."
- "I make my living training departments within corporations to communicate better, and I do a good job—but I have to be hyper-prepared and it's agony. I have to know everything I'm going to say a week before I say it, and rehearse endlessly. I just want to be relaxed and comfortable with those people. I want to be spontaneous."
- "I hold back at church or PTA because I'm not quite sure what I want to say, and I'm afraid people won't listen anyway. When I do have to stand up and report on a committee, I just go as fast as I can to get it over."

Which kind of speaker are you?

- Are you confident addressing a group when you know exactly what you are going to say, but lose presence when you need to be spontaneous?
- Can you run a meeting or training session with great spontaneity and excitement, but go stiff and dull when asked to present a prepared talk?
- Does the prospect of standing in front of any group fill you with feelings of dread, discomfort, shyness, anxiety, or trepidation—even though you know in your heart you have a contribution to make?

- Are you already a good speaker who could use some leading-edge coaching to take you over the top?
- Are you some combination of the above?

I have tested this process in more than 2,000 groups over 7 years with CEOs, sales people, entrepreneurs, trainers, school-children, artists and writers, storytellers, community leaders, health care professionals, and others from every walk of life, as well as with professional speakers. I believe it can turn almost anyone into a relaxed, charismatic speaker who actually enjoys being in front of groups and can communicate a clear message with high impact—just by being themselves.

Whether you use it for creative self-expression, professional development, or both, you will learn more about yourself and enhance your ability to share your message with others.

Confidence with public speaking carries over into all aspects of personal and professional life. Transformational Speaking takes you to the next level, whether you aspire to be a $50,000-a-date speaker like management consultant Tom Peters, address your staff for 5 minutes with your head held high, or inspire friends over lunch.

Speaking as life

Transformational Speaking is about the thrill of self-discovery, stepping into the creative unknown, and allowing ourselves the luxury of giving and receiving unconditional positive support from other people.

It puts us in the middle of life's adventure. We find what is unique about ourselves, and also discover our deepest connections and commonalities with other people. "I've learned more about myself and other people, and about where we touch each other, in 3 weeks in a Speaking Circle than I did in 20 years of studying psychology and metaphysics," said one writer.

Speaking Circles let us do on a small scale what we all want to do in the world: share support and community, and in the process find more of ourselves.

And as in life, we already have within us everything we need to be Transformational Speakers; it's just a matter of bringing our talents, powers, and essence to the surface.

In the next few chapters, we will explore specific aspects of Transformational Speaking. But first, let's look at how this new kind of speaking is different from the old paradigm. ◎

Chapter 2

Old Myths, New Paradigm

We all want to be heard more often, and more fully—whether we are speaking to a boss, partner, potential client, family member, friend, or to a large group. In an age of information overload and short attention spans, that's becoming increasingly difficult.

A lot of the old messages aren't getting through. Both corporate America and individuals who want authentic, respectful relationships are moving away from hierarchical structures, manipulation, power-tripping, coercion, and artificial "communication techniques."

We are looking for ways to connect and work with one another that are compassionate, productive, and life-enhancing. We want to capture people's attention more quickly and touch them more deeply, in both our personal and professional lives. That's exactly what Transformational Speaking gives us.

The new paradigm

Transformational Speakers know that *to be heard now, you have to be here now.*

That brings a whole new dimension to what happens when one person speaks and other people listen. We speak from a deeper place within ourselves, in present time, and give a priority to connecting on a human level that commands people's attention and support. It is a catalyst for making things happen in business and enriching personal relationships.

But when most of us hear the words "public speaking," that's not what comes to mind. This powerful new paradigm is changing how we interact with one another and think about public speaking on five fronts.

1. OLD MYTH: Public speaking is about mastering PERFORMANCE and winning the audience over with style and technique.

NEW PARADIGM: Public speaking is about EXPRESSION of our authentic selves.

When speaking is a performance, then the audience is watching a performer or actor—not necessarily a person who is relating from his or her authentic self. An invisible curtain always keeps this performer a certain distance from the audience. Performance requires a script, rehearsals, and lots of effort. It traps the performer in a prescribed set of "Do"s and "Don't"s. He can only go so far toward his own truth, or toward the audience.

Magic happens when we approach speaking from the perspective of expressing ourselves, and not performing. When speaking is the natural expression of what we believe and live, then our audience is spending time with a human being who is telling his or her own truth. Our passion becomes infectious. We can relax, and so the people listening to us can relax.

One Circle Speaker said it was like being an artist: "The air space is my canvas and I am the brush."

The new paradigm turns *automated* public speakers into *authentic* speakers, and Circle Speakers list authenticity first among all the benefits of Transformational Speaking.

- "Speaking Circles helped break me out of a formula style of speaking into a much more lively, natural, and personally enjoyable way of presenting my ideas," said a psychologist who lectures across the country.
- "When I'm being most myself on stage, I can actually feel the audience being touched by me," said a corporate trainer.
- "There's a quality created in the room when a speaker is authentically present, and it just comes down to one word: love," a software CEO told me.

- "What a relief to find that I could be more effective by speaking to the audience in my natural style, directly from my heart and belly, rather than according to the teachings of traditional public speaking classes," wrote a business consultant and author.
- "Exploring expression in front of a group allows me to connect my heart to my theories, and to discover why the things I speak and write about are important to me," a novelist said.
- "Speaking is the art of engagement! It is every bit as exciting and transformative as other arts. I've begun expressing myself creatively through it in ways I hadn't even imagined," said a woman who owns an art gallery.

2. *OLD MYTH: Stage fright must be conquered and overcome.*
NEW PARADIGM: Stage fright must be honored and moved through.

Anxiety on stage, or in any spotlight, is normal and healthy. We can try covering it up with techniques and exacting preparation, which is what people usually try to do, sometimes with a degree of success—but this keeps us from ever making a real heart connection with our listeners.

The way to move through stage fright organically, to dissolve it rather than just to mask it, is *to stand before a supportive group and let ourselves* feel *the fear.* We may even want to talk about it.

This accomplishes two things. First, we are no longer fighting the fear. Whenever we resist something we are feeling, it becomes like a beach ball that we're trying to hold underwater. We can push it down again and again, but the minute we relax our grip, it springs to the surface and makes a big splash. When we stop resisting the fear, we stop giving it power. We stop making it strong by providing it with something to push against.

Second, when we allow ourselves to feel our fear in front of a supportive group who would never do all the terrible things we're (consciously or unconsciously) afraid they are going to do to us, we start breaking down our belief that there is something to fear.

When a group beams appreciative attention to someone with stage fright, the fear usually melts away—and is often replaced by an absolute joy and a new expressiveness that comes as much from relief as it does from receiving the support. When the fear honestly disappears, rather than just getting covered up, we can move more deeply into our own wisdom and reach out more directly to the audience—even an audience in the "real world" that has not agreed to be unconditionally supportive.

Here is what two Transformational Speakers had to say about stage fright:

- "I've been speaking to large groups for 15 years and have always had a big fear of drawing a blank. With support, I've discovered that when I don't know what to say next, I can just take a few seconds 'in the void.' Something always comes—and when I see myself on videotape, that silence looks fine. As a result, I have created a whole new, and more honest, relationship with my audiences."

- "I started out terrified to show my real self. It's a natural fear for those of us who have suffered some crushing event, but I've learned to open up and talk about what excites me in life."

3. OLD MYTH: Public speaking is a task with defined parameters.
NEW PARADIGM: Public speaking is an art with infinite possibilities.

The traditional motivation for improving our communication in front of groups is professional development, whether in the service of becoming a paid speaker or a more effective business leader. A new view is that by learning how to express ourselves better in public, we can enrich our lives and open up new options, both personally and professionally.

Finding the "Inner Speaker" is a delicious and transforming process that helps us know ourselves better, work through difficulties we have in connecting with others, get clearer on what we believe, and find a stronger voice to express those beliefs in all areas of our lives.

Circle Speakers talk about the place speaking holds in their lives:

- "Speaking is my meditation. It's how I grow, and what I use as my focus for expanding internally."

- "Speaking has become for me a transformational experience. Every time I get up on stage and hold the microphone, I learn more about myself. I grow, and I'm pushed to say what I believe. We all have a particular knowledge, and I believe we're put on earth to speak that truth."

- "Expressing myself on stage with support allows me to synthesize my ideas, thoughts, and experiences until sparks fly and I am amazed at what comes out of my mouth. I am learning what my unique gift is by sharing it. This clarity gives me more self-confidence in *everything* I do, not just speaking."

- "Speaking for me is learning to play, to have a conversation and not know where it's going, and to just somehow tune into that inner frequency that's always there. There's always something going on, and if we can just keep our antennas tuned in, it's amazing what we find. It's like keeping my pilot light on."

4. OLD MYTH: Humor is about making *people laugh.*
NEW PARADIGM: Humor is about letting *people laugh.*

Humor that is mean-spirited, deprecating, manipulating, or coerced from an audience isn't funny for very long.

Healthy and effective humor comes out of sharing an awareness of our common humanity—our weaknesses and frailties, the tension in our relationships, the chatter of our minds. Laughter flows when we remember that the human mind is God's practical joke, and when we share the embarrassment of being human—together.

Several participants in Speaking Circles have been humorists and storytellers, and many others have turned *into* humorists and storytellers:

- "People laugh at the most unexpected places when I'm telling stories about my life. I'm at my funniest when I'm really not trying to be funny but am just having a good time recounting something that happened."

- "As a humorist, when I share my humanity and emotions I am gently massaging the listeners' pain until it turns to pleasure, like when someone tenderly pushes and rubs the crick in your back."

- "As we get older and wiser, we find out more of who we've always been. It's sort of like a banana, peeling off some of those defense mechanisms and expressing what's underneath. Drama is about peeling the onion; comedy is about peeling the banana."

5. *OLD MYTH: Critical feedback spurs improvement.*
NEW PARADIGM: Positive feedback nurtures growth.

Too many speaking careers are sabotaged in the early stages by what marketing expert and direct mail copy writer David Garfinkel calls the "friendly fire" of well-meaning suggestions from friends and associates in the guise of "advice," "helpful criticism," and "the honest truth"—"truths" like:

- "I counted five 'um's in your talk."
- "You speak too fast."
- "You seemed nervous."
- "You might try walking across the stage and gesturing like so to drive home that point."

David and I were business partners for several years in developing and applying some of these key concepts in the world of professional speaking. He believes that later on in professional development, as speakers refine their craft, sensitively delivered direct criticism is not only useful, but necessary.

But I have found that speakers at *any* stage of professional development make quantum leaps in self-expression when they get generous amounts of support and appreciation—and that critical "corrections" are not only paralyzing, but often inaccurate. In Speaking Circles, we only invite positive feedback—and people flourish. There is no need to be shamed in public in order to know what you want to correct.

Transformational Speaking represents not only a new way of speaking, but a new way of relating, living, and doing business. In the next chapter, we'll go inside a Speaking Circle to see this new paradigm in action. ◎

Chapter 3

Inside the Speaking Circle

"Expect magic, surprises, laughter, joy, insight, and inspiration when you go to a Speaking Circle," a management consultant tells people. "For $30, you get 2½ hours of great theater, and then you get to go up on stage yourself!"

(Of course you can save the $30 by growing your own Speaking Circle among colleagues and/or friends. See Chapter 17.)

Speaking Circles run on an energy that is free, non-polluting, completely enlivening, and infinite. It's called human support, and it can bring out the latent super-speaker in everyone.

This chapter describes what we do in Circles, and explains the principles on which they work.

What does a Circle look like?

Each Circle has its own character, logistics, look, and "feel." I believe ten people is as large as a Circle should get. One reason is that, with any more, the Circle lasts more than 2½ hours—and that's too long for most of us to stay fully engaged.

We sit either in a circle or theater style, sometimes with a small riser or platform in front of the room. Most Circles have a video-tape camera set up in the back, operated by the facilitator.

When we arrive, we greet one another, get some tea or coffee, and find a seat. The facilitator opens the Circle with a short "hello" share and reviews the Speaking Circle principles and agenda:

1. Everyone gives the speaker unconditional support and positive acceptance—silently while the person is speaking, and with positive comments during feedback time.

2. The speaker receives that support, letting in the positive attention, applause, or comments from the group.

3. We don't talk among ourselves during or between speakers, or comment on the content of people's talks (what was said, rather than how it was said).

4. We go around the circle once so that everyone can stand in front of the room to "check in" for 3 minutes, with no feedback. Then each person gets up and has 5 minutes to talk, connect in silence, or do whatever he or she wants with that time. This is followed by brief, positive feedback. (Each person brings his or her own videotape each week, and the 3-minute "check in," the 5 minutes, and the feedback are all taped.)

As the facilitator gives this four-part introduction, he or she models the support and safety that are the foundation of Speaking Circles. No matter what is going on in his or her own life, participants get 100% attention and positive regard. The facilitator looks for the best in each person, for the inner beauty and strength that are finding their way to the surface, and genuinely supports that part of each participant in emerging. After the ground rules and logistics are covered, the facilitator pauses before leaving the platform to accept the group's applause and goodwill.

Then one by one, we get 3 minutes in front of the room to check in, say hello, share where we are, and "get here." Some people "check in" in silence, slowly being with one person, then another, and another—receiving each person's support and acceptance. These 3 minutes are simply a chance to get present in the room.

Then we start around the circle again, and each person has 5 minutes to do whatever we want: speak about something we've planned to discuss, talk about whatever pops into our heads, sing, talk about our lives, or stand in the silence. Whatever we do, or don't do, we get unconditional support and positive regard from the audience. At the end of 5 minutes, the facilitator asks us how it was for us, then we get positive feedback from the group about what they felt and experienced while we were in front of the room.

After everyone has had their three minutes, their five minutes, and their feedback, the facilitator closes the Circle with a short wrap-up. With ten people, the Circle takes about 2½ hours—and people usually spend a little time afterward catching up with one another, building friendship and community.

The safest room on earth

The most important thing about the Speaking Circle is that it is *safe*. Judgments, criticism, competition, and anything other than wholehearted support are left at the door. We all get to have our say, and to be supported. This safety, the foundation of Speaking Circles, is what allows people to relax into their essence.

"We learn to focus on what is *right* in people," says a motivational speaker who has been coming to Circles for years. "You're in the riskiest situation possible—speaking in public—and you find out that you don't have to alter your basic self in order to survive. In fact, the more I'm myself, the better it turns out. That changed everything for me. It showed me I could trust myself just to relax and be wherever I was in my life!"

A psychologist says, "The safety lets us take risks, and that is where we find ourselves—in that risk-taking. That's where the magic happens, and where people blossom and unfold. An unexplainable presence gets activated when people come together as witnesses to one another in that safe environment."

Our truest selves come out when it is safe. When people were interviewed for this book, "Safety" ranked highest on the list of what made people feel more spontaneous, creative, and confident. Michael Toms, co-founder of New Dimensions Radio, wrote, "I found myself in a safe space among peers, which allowed me to be authentic. Not only that—no small accomplishment—I came away with tools and insights to enable me to take that authenticity into daily life."

When we get complete support for whatever we do, and who-ever we are, we can drop our defenses and trust the group. *That lets us stretch our limits* while continuing to build on our strengths. When we see over and over that we can be ourselves without any-thing bad happening, we start to become more and more authen-tic. When the group's assumption is that we communicate well, we start to communicate even better.

Transpersonal counselor Evie Belove, founder of the women's support group Celebrate Menopause, says:

> I've always been externally oriented, always looking around to see what was okay to say to this person, to this group. I tailored everything I said for my listeners. Speak-ing Circles have helped me to just be me and say whatever I have to say. It's like I can't make a mistake, and now I sud-denly feel expansive in my expression.
>
> If you want something to grow, you put it in the sun-shine. If you want a person to grow, you put them in the sun of love and support. There aren't many places where people are safe today, but this is one of them.

A social worker told me she is patterning all her relationships after the safety she finds in Speaking Circles. "It's an awesome experience to have total support without any criticism. If my hus-band and I have something to say to one another now, we say it in a loving and supportive way."

Speaking Circle safety has three sources: the facilitator, the au-dience, and the speaker.

Being the facilitator

Gayla Alders facilitates a Speaking Circle in Marin County just north of San Francisco. In addition to her regular Circles, she has worked with Marin AIDS projects and will be starting Circles in San Quentin. She gives a good description of what the facilitator does, in form and substance.

> I'm just there to make it safe for everyone. To make sure people give the speaker their full attention, to have people really take in the applause after they speak, and to make sure all the feedback is positive, and that they talk about what they *felt* as people spoke. If I model those things, if I have a supportive, receiving, positive attitude, then the participants will do it, too.
>
> I'm not a teacher. In Circles, I'm the one who learns. I get to live in the light that people give off as more and more of their essence emerges. My job is to just get out of the way and let the evening come out of them. It's like ice skating. Every person is different, and we all have to find our own edge on the skates. My job is to make it safe enough for them to experiment and find their edge.

Being in the audience

Many people say that being in the audience improves their speaking just as much as being in front of the room does.

In the audience, our job is to give our full attention and support to the speaker. We see that person as a work of art, as a unique expression of Life, and tune into his or her inner beauty. That feels good!

Even if we don't have much instinctive appreciation of a particular person, we know that we'll have an opportunity to give positive feedback in a few minutes—so we learn to *look* for something we like. After a while, most people recognize that when we feel critical of someone, we're usually just reacting to something in the speaker that reminds us of a part of ourselves we haven't embraced, or that reminds us of someone with whom we have difficulties.

When we move away from being judgmental and focus instead on what is likable about that person, we usually feel enormous relief and even elation. The ability to make this shift can be extremely valuable, both in business and in our personal relationships.

"I remember there was this one woman who just pushed my buttons," says a professor at the University of California at Berkeley. "I found it really hard to support her, but then I realized that in a few minutes I'd have a chance to give some positive feedback about her. So I started looking for things I liked, and by the time she was finished I found I actually did like her. She's turned out to be a close friend."

It's much more pleasant to enjoy and support people than it is to sit and stew critically about everything that's wrong with them. In Circles, we practice this refocusing to the positive over and over until it becomes part of our daily lives. When people are around us, they can make mistakes and still be beautiful. They can flounder until they find an inner truth. They can be defenseless, without a practiced technical style, until they find their own natural dance in front of the room. They can be appreciated and embraced, warts and all, in all their richness and humanity.

When we can give other people those opportunities, we enjoy life more and people want to be around us. We're operating from the best part of ourselves, and that's ultimately what most of us want to do in life.

"We're looking for the light in everyone who stands up there, not for the shadow," says a legal secretary. "And as we give them permission to be just the way they are, we give ourselves that same permission."

Supporting other people also gives us a new perspective on our own audiences. We realize that audiences are not mere stand-ins for the disapproving adults whom we encountered as children, but real human beings who want to support us as much as we want to support other people.

"I always thought people in the audience were judging me to death," says an attorney. "But in Circles the audience is not there to judge you. I have a very active inner critic, but when I'm sitting in the Circle audience, I can and want to support people. I know it's easier when the speaker *accepts* my support—so when I'm the speaker, I try to open up and receive what the audience is giving me. The more I do it with these people, the easier it is to do outside."

We human beings are actually very good at giving support. It comes naturally, and we enjoy doing it—especially when there are time limits and we only have to maintain that absolute support for 5 minutes. Almost everyone can give that much support.

Being the speaker

When it's our turn to be in front of the room, our priority is simply to *receive* support from the audience.

We rarely have a chance to be the center of attention with the absolute assurance that people will support us no matter what we do or don't do. This is a unique opportunity to explore how much of that attention and support we are willing to take in.

Before we begin talking, we spend a few moments in silence noticing individuals in the audience. We receive the support from one person for 5 to 10 seconds, exploring the connection, and then we move on to another person. We don't have to look at everyone in the audience. We just want to center ourselves in our relationship with a few people, and that bond will spread to everyone.

Ideally, whatever we say comes out of the relationship we're building with the group—and is as intimate and real as a conversation we might have with a close friend. As we speak, we stay in constant connection with one individual in the audience, then another and another, keeping eye connection with each person for about 5 to 10 seconds. When we let natural silences fall, we still stay connected to one individual at a time—and we let what we say next, and how we say it, come out of that connection.

We may feel tight or nervous, or have voices in our heads asking, "What am I going to say?" We may find ourselves scanning our mental Rolodex for something to talk about, or we may draw a blank. Most of those things do happen at some point. We just notice them, and keep receiving people's support. We don't judge those feelings, or get nervous about being nervous. We just let ourselves be, and we may even talk about our discomfort. People sometimes say, "I can't believe I'm so nervous up here," or "I can't believe I have no idea what to say and I'm *not* nervous," or "I'm drawing a blank." We just keep going back to receiving, and to the connection, and let everything that happens grow out of that.

People occasionally have some idea of what they are going to say, or at least where they'll start, but most like to be surprised. "When I first started coming, I would *plan* what I was going to say—but now I know the magic happens when I *don't* plan," says an engineer. "Last week I thought I was going to talk about one thing and it wound up being something totally different—and I learned a lot about myself. I can drop down into my heart now, instead of always coming from the head, as engineers have been conditioned to do."

As we learn to open our hearts to the audience, we begin to see a world of support shining through their eyes. Performance anxiety begins to dissolve. The habit of rushing our words and thoughts drops away. We can trust that we are appreciated for exactly who we are, not for what we do or say.

Then the words flow naturally from our hearts without fear or hesitation.

Positive feedback

After we've had our 5 minutes in front of the room, the people in the group give concise (usually 10 to 20 seconds), positive feedback about how it felt to share that time with us. They do not give suggestions, critiques, advice, comments on the content of what we said, or comparisons to other talks we've given—just positive feedback about their experience of our essence and our connection with the group.

They would *not* say, for example:

- "That was great, but I'd put your story about your mother first."
- "You were so much more alive this time!"
- "I knew someone with that same problem, and he found that..."

Sometimes the feedback is as creative and magical as what people do in front of the room:

- "It was like popcorn and confetti."
- "Being with you was like swimming in a river of chocolate."
- "It reminded me of a perfume I used to wear: intriguing and on the edge."

No matter where people begin, they make quantum leaps in self-expression when they receive generous appreciation and positive feedback—whereas the learning curve plummets when shame becomes part of the process.

"I hated all that positive feedback and applause at first," the manager of an electronics store told me. "I thought, 'They're full of it.' I had a lot of self-judgment. The next time I tried to say, 'No, no,' but I *wanted* it. My mind was running a number, but my gut was saying, 'Hey, this feels good.'"

As speakers, it's important that we really *hear* the positive feedback and *take it in*—for ourselves and for the people in the audience. They are giving us a gift, and it pains them when we refuse to receive it.

"We're taught to look for what's wrong," said a contractor who has been coming to Circles for 2 years. "We look for differences and things that bother us; we're not trained to *accentuate the hon-*

est positive. Sometimes it's hard to receive honest praise, but if we don't, we do a disservice to ourselves and the other people."

Sometimes it takes practice to receive positive feedback. "I'd never had 8 minutes of undivided attention before in my life," said one woman. "It was delicious, but it took some getting used to."

A court reporter told me, "Positive feedback is what let me start believing I had something to say. I don't need negative feedback because I'll take care of that myself. After a while, when I got the same thing from many people, my self-consciousness evaporated. I was more myself, and that's what people like the best."

Just as miracles happen through positive feedback, I've seen very painful situations evolve when this guideline was ignored and people gave negative, or even neutral, feedback. I've also found that negative feedback is almost always highly inaccurate, and that it usually reflects an agenda on the part of the person who gives it.

One woman asked her midwestern Circle of professional speakers to put the guideline aside "just this once" so that she could get some "realistic feedback" on what to do with one of her stories. They agreed, but the minute they started giving objective evaluation—nothing said was particularly negative—she fell apart. She understood immediately why this guideline is so important. It's difficult, and perhaps not even a good idea, to become very vulnerable when people may critique what you say or do—no matter how gentle, kind, or well-meaning that feedback is.

Positive feedback is becoming a business tool. Saul Eisen is a Speaking Circle veteran and professor of Organization Development at Sonoma State University who trains consultants and teaches in the MBA Program.

> I help people change their organizations so that they are more effective and more human. The "Appreciative Inquiry" approach developed by David Cooperrider is very similar to Speaking Circles. They've discovered that if you go into an organization and only talk about the problems, everyone just gets depressed. But if you talk about what's working well, people do more of that and everyone gets excited.

> We aren't brought up to be comfortable with positive
> feedback. We're supposed to brush off compliments and be
> embarrassed, but once people start believing and accepting
> it, and really let it in, it's very freeing. The plant you water
> is the plant that will grow.

Receiving positive feedback lets us experience warmer and more
trusting connections with others, witness the good in ourselves,
and open to new levels of love and power—in front of the room,
and in life.

Love, truth, and video tape

The first time most people watch their tapes, all they see is what
they *don't* like: their nose, their hair, that extra 15 pounds, all the
"bad" things they did when they spoke, the "um"s and "ah"s. The
negative voices inside their heads have a field day.

I always suggest that people watch their first tapes at least three
times. That takes us beyond the negativity and voices, and we
begin to see what's actually there. We see the beauty and vulnerability of our real selves, and the strength of our own voice emerging. Those things may be in an embryonic state at first, but we
can see them and start to build on them.

Things we want to eliminate seem to fall away naturally, without much effort—often without our even being consciously aware
of them. People who didn't even know that they had some distracting habits or were using a lot of "Ya know"s automatically let
these things go without even realizing they had them in the first
place.

Tapes also reveal the inner beauty that comes of telling our
truth, whatever that may be. A business writer remembers,

> I'd had one of those totally rotten days and felt just
> awful—pissed off at everybody and angry. When I got up to
> speak, I just let myself just be there. It blew off some of the
> anger, but I was sure it had been a terrible thing to see and
> resisted watching the tape.

> But a week later when I finally watched the tape, I saw a
> guy who was *real*. There was a lot of energy, and that guy

was present with what was going on with him. Over time, I've learned that the times I thought I was being my worst, because the real me was coming out, I was actually being my best.

The tapes also show how a natural clarity emerges in people's thinking when they just let themselves explore a topic or problem in front of the room without preparing what they say. They wind down one path, and then down another, and suddenly, usually in a very magical way, the two paths come together and everything makes sense intuitively and organically. Solutions seem to pop out of nowhere. Our inner wisdom emerges when we're willing to hang out with people in "not knowing."

Often, someone in a Circle does something so good that I'm sure it's scripted. But when I ask them if they prepared their talk, they say, "Oh, I was just rambling; I don't even know what I said." Later, when they go home and watch the tape, they are amazed how it all came together and made sense.

People who never thought they had much of a "voice" emerge as wonderful storytellers, and storytellers who attend Circles become "super natural" tale spinners. Video aids this process by giving us a chance to compare our internal experience to our external experience. It almost always looks a lot better than we think it's going to look, and frees us to shed another layer of self-consciousness when we speak next.

A psychologist and Speaking Circle veteran agrees: "When I finally gather the courage to view what feels emotionally like a 'dud' talk, I realize it is never as bad as it feels inside. I know how I see the world, but the video shows me how I look to others. Usually I'm much too harsh with myself, and look a lot better than those critical inner voices are telling me I look."

Videotape gives us perspective on ourselves—and it's almost always a better perspective than our inner critic gives us.

Fat furry worms that fly

Speaking Circles are full of miracles and transformation, and the magic carries over into our lives. We are the same people outside Speaking Circles as we are inside them, and we take the skills, insights, and appreciation of ourselves and others that we learn in Circles out into our work and our relationships. People keep coming back every week not only because their public speaking or communication at work improve, but also because their connections with themselves and with the people in their lives keep getting richer and richer.

Butterflies are a symbol of change, of metamorphosis into something larger and more beautiful. Yet we all know that butterflies begin as caterpillars, fat furry worms, and that they need time, safety, and nurturing to evolve into the magnificence that is coded into their DNA.

Many people have told me they consider Speaking Circles the cocoon that let them emerge into their natural power and full voice. As change happens more and more quickly in our world, and we all have to change more quickly to survive and thrive, we need people and processes that support us in evolving into butterflies—again and again.

Speaking Circles give us not only that safety and support, but a graduate program in adjusting to change. We are constantly renewing our connections with one another minute to minute, and being present in this unique moment in time. Circles also give us ongoing practice in experiencing our fear of change, and going through it anyway—over and over again.

Speaking Circle veteran, singer, and songwriter Jana Stanfield of Nashville wrote this song about change, with Joyce Rouse.

Butterfly

Sitting alone on a hillside confused about what to do
My choices were all complicated, it was time to think
    things through
Spotted a striped caterpillar stretching her face to the sky
Dragging her cumbersome body an inch at a time
I was feeling the pain of slow progress when a friend of
    hers fluttered by
I leaned close as the caterpillar spoke with a voice as soft
    as a sigh.
She said,

(Chorus)
Butterfly, please tell me again I'm gonna be alright
I can feel a change is coming
I can feel it in my skin
I can feel myself outgrowing
This life I've been living in
And I'm afraid, afraid of change
Butterfly, please tell me again I'm gonna be alright.

I'm like my friend caterpillar, afraid of that dark cocoon
Wanting to hide in the tall grass, when change is coming
    soon
But all of the things that we long for are borne on the
    wings of change
And losses can lead us to blessings that we can't explain
Butterflies remind us, there's magic in every life
And we can become what we dream of, if fat furry worms
    can fly.
So I say, *(Chorus)*

And on the day of my last breath
I expect to see angels like butterflies over my head.
And I'll say, *(Chorus)*

Each Speaking Circle is absolutely unique. Certain specific people come together in that particular way, on that given day.

What will your Circle look like? Chapter 17 is about how to set up your own Circle, and we have prepared a videotape to help you do this. You can order the tape by sending in the order form at the back of this book. ◉

Chapter 4

Healing the Inner Speaker

Why don't we all just step up to the front of the room, embrace the audience with our presence, receive their support, and speak in clear, heartfelt ways that change people's lives?

Why do we have to *practice* relaxing, being ourselves, and receiving from other people?

Why we shut down

Very few of us assume that if we are just ourselves, we will be supported—and that's because most of us *weren't* supported for simply being ourselves when we were children.

In fact, most of us were taught *not* to relax and be ourselves—and that message was reinforced in school, in business, and in society. We've learned to cover up our essence with masks, personas, internal walls, and "style." Sometimes these defenses give us the illusion of feeling safer or stronger, and when performed well may even contribute to a modicum of professional success. But they limit our connections with people and put a ceiling on our potential effectiveness—and they are no fun.

Most of us learn to edit ourselves early in life. It's the nature of children to do things that are not socially acceptable, especially in public—throwing food on the wall, screaming at odd moments, interrupting, saying embarrassing things about how people look, or expressing negative opinions about birthday presents from Grandma. Part of being socialized is learning not to do these things.

Most parents deliver the message loud and clear, and as children we can't always distinguish between what is Real And Not Okay, and what is Real But Okay.

Sometimes being real *was* okay with our parents. We were probably given positive attention for our endearing smiles, or the time we spontaneously hugged Uncle Albert, or presented Grandma with a hand-made 80th birthday card—but on the whole, being real involved a lot of negative feedback. Many of us gave up the rewards to avoid the punishment.

If we grew up with adults whose self-worth depended on how their children looked in public, or who needed perfect children in order to prove that they were perfect parents, then we may have trouble being real in front of groups. Being perfect and being real are almost always at odds. If we tried to be perfect, we probably couldn't be very real.

These early incidents didn't always involve punishment. We may have been laughed at, ridiculed, or ignored. Kids are prone to say things that adults find funny. If we announced at age 5, for instance, that we were going to be a nuclear physicist or a martyred saint, we may have given everybody a good laugh. But from our point of view, we were being ridiculed for being honest and vulnerable—and we learned to be careful. We learned to edit, and in many cases to keep our true selves and our true feelings under wraps.

If we let fly with a piece of our authentic selves and were punished or ridiculed, then we have a reasonable fear of being ourselves in public. People have told me that when they look out into an audience, they often see a disapproving parent or adult—multiplied by five, ten, fifty, or however many people are sitting out there. Psychologists say that whenever more than two people come together in a group, we are consciously or unconsciously involved in a family dynamic.

So every time we get in front of a room, we are exposing ourselves to a punishing family dynamic in public. No wonder we get nervous, shut down, become stiff, panic, tremble, get dry throat, put ourselves "on catatonic automatic," memorize every word we're going to say so we'll feel a little in control, or adopt masks, oratorical postures, personas, and cavalier "styles" that make us seem impervious to criticism. All of these things protect, and disconnect, us from our audience.

In a threatening situation, our instinct is to defend ourselves. The last thing we want to do is open up and make ourselves vulnerable to those people. If we see them as the powerful adults whose "guidance," criticism, or outright abuse hurt us when we were small, then we're inviting trouble if we let ourselves relax.

The wounded speaker

The wound occurred when we stopped trusting ourselves, and being ourselves. Our parents and other adults probably did not mean to inflict those wounds, but despite their good intentions, we started to deny or hide our real selves. We may even have started believing that the edited, stunted person we pretended to be was who we really were.

Therapist and Speaking Circle veteran Margaret Reardon of San Francisco says,

> My orientation is that we all experience early relationships in ways that impact us later on, and those experiences can be wounding. We're always told how *not* to do things, but we're not told what's good or wonderful about what we do. In Speaking Circles, all the positive attention may feel narcissistic at first, but it shores us up and this is the healing—being able to look at ourselves objectively and see the good things as well. We learn to see that we really can relax into ourselves and be real—and that people find that both fascinating and lovable.

Healing the wound

Most of us have learned to be authentic one-on-one, but it takes practice to be real in public. Our Inner Speakers are wounded, and the dynamics of Speaking Circles are the perfect way to heal this particular wound.

Our primary instruction as Transformational Speakers is to explore receiving the group's support and positive acknowledgment. As we do that again and again, we start moving beyond our fears that people will be bored, punishing, or derisive. We open up to the good will that is actually there for us, and to people's appreciation of who we are. We experience being completely seen and fully supported exactly the way we are, and reverse the wounding process by getting positive, rather than negative, reinforcement for being ourselves.

"I've realized that getting up in front of an audience is my way of healing a lot of wounds, of overcoming years of not being heard in my personal life, and being criticized constantly," said one teacher who has been coming to Circles for a year. "I know I won't be told what's 'wrong' with me. It's great to be able to take risks and not feel uneasy."

Another way that Speaking Circles help us heal is that we can talk about those painful early experience, which releases a lot of the energy behind them. One therapist said:

> I was terrified in the Circle at first, but I was also receiving something there that I'd never had. I was being completely listened to, and seen as who I actually was. That helped me work through a lot of issues about who my parents told me I was. To have people really listen and just accept whatever I said was a revelation. The first year I was in tears a lot, and I found a different voice. I began to speak so quietly...the room would be dead silent. All my life, I'd been trying to speak up, to be heard, and people told me to pipe down. But in the Circle, as my voice got quieter and quieter, it commanded more and more attention.

In Speaking Circles, we can let ourselves feel the old fears—and also know that nobody will criticize, interrupt, or psychoanalyze us. No one will take over the conversation or quip, "Cat got your tongue?" No one will imply that there's something wrong with us, try to fix us, or put us on the spot. We are honored for whatever we say, or don't say. It's our time, and our space to be completely appreciated. That is the healing.

Sooner or later, usually sooner, the fears and defenses lift away naturally. It's not that we never feel wounded or fearful again, but we are senior to those experiences and they don't stop us.

Wound in public, heal in public

Therapist Hal Perry recalls a specific incident that started to heal in Speaking Circles.

> I had been speaking in public for years, but always at the cost of enormous anxiety and energy. I was so overprepared that I would have every word of the talk written out and could recite.
>
> I realized that it all stemmed from an incident when I was twenty and going away to college. The church gave me a party and the pastor said complimentary things about me. Then he asked me to come up and say a few words. I was so overcome with emotion that I burst into tears and couldn't stop crying. It was a devastating experience, because I'd never seen a grown man cry in public. From that moment on, public speaking was an agonizing experience—even when I knew the material well and wanted to share it.
>
> At my first Speaking Circle I realized that this was the place to heal that early incident that had caused me so much anxiety over the years. After attending a few times, I had the courage to share this experience in a Speaking Circle talk. Being able to tell the truth about my vulnerability, and getting that rapt attention, caring, love, and acceptance started to melt the energy around that incident and minimize the power it had over me.

When I gave my next professional talk a few months later, I wasn't even nervous the day before. I had always been so wrapped up in my own anxiety that I hardly paid any attention to the audience. Now I actually enjoy speaking, and can relax and relate more easily to the people in the audience.

Most of us have an incident or incidents that form the basis of our discomfort with speaking in public. Speaking Circles are an opportunity to heal them.

The magic of being fully seen and heard

When we feel fully seen and heard, supported, and given positive regard—it acts as a salve to the Inner Speaker's wound. We can think and breathe, and we become whole again. We get reacquainted with ourselves, and bring ourselves more fully and more genuinely out into the world. Sometimes this healing happens the first time someone stands up; sometimes it takes longer. But eventually, the wound is bound to heal in the loving, positive, supportive environment of the Circle.

After this healing has occurred, nothing is ever the same. We have a part of ourselves that we didn't have before. We are whole in public, and so we can share ourselves with others without fear.

"I'm glad Speaking Circles are starting in the schools," says one teacher. "We aren't accustomed to being listened to in our society, and we feel invisible a lot of the time. We run around trying to get attention—sometimes in ways that aren't very productive. When we feel fully heard, we can drop all those bells and whistles. If kids realized earlier that they aren't invisible, we'd have a better chance of educating them. It's very simple work, but it's very important and deep."

"Imagine if you had this kind of support at a family dinner table," said a Circle facilitator, "if everybody got even 2 minutes of attention and support to be wherever they were and say whatever they wanted. Imagine children raised with that amount of respect."

This kind of inner work enhances all our relationships. We human beings simply cannot resist another full, genuine human being who is at ease with himself and fully expressive—and we can only relate to other people like that when we've healed our Inner Speaker.

Growing in the greenhouse

Professional artist George Allen Durkee sees Speaking Circles as the greenhouse where we experience special, particularly favorable conditions in which to heal and grow.

If you take even the sickest plant and put it in a greenhouse with perfect conditions—ideal amounts of moisture, light, and temperature—it will start to flourish. It will straighten up, and start to produce new shoots. It will get well, and start to be creative. Speaking Circles are a chance to come in out of the cold or darkness we may experience at work or at home, and nourish ourselves in ideal conditions for a few hours a week. We begin to heal, and grow new shoots. We discover that we have the potential to produce beautiful flowers. When it's safe to stretch, we find out what we can do.

When you can do anything you want in front of the room—be outrageous, be depressed, even hide—and still get those perfect conditions, you not only heal, you begin to see what you really *want* to say and do. You get in touch with your real voice, and what you really have to say to people. When we have unlimited options, we go naturally to the ones that have the most resonance for us. That's another level of healing, to find our true voice and what we really have to say about life.

When plants have had some time in the greenhouse to heal and grow, they can go back out into the world and be strong. In the same way, we take our learning and healing from the Speaking Circles back out into our lives. We're stronger, we know ourselves better, we're more real, and we can allow more support into our lives.

The air inside this special greenhouse is made of equal parts safety and support, relaxing and receiving.

What the mirror tells us

In Speaking Circles, the audience acts as a mirror, reflecting back the beautiful parts of us so that we can see them—often for the first time. This heals the wound inflicted when we didn't have those wonderful parts of ourselves reflected back to us as children.

"I learned how to be present to myself in Circles, rather than being concerned about the content or the words I was saying," says a healer. "With relating and breathing, looking into people's eyes and receiving, I get a much better take on what's going on inside me."

When people are in front of the room, they often come to a sudden understanding of what is important in their lives. Sometimes they have never spoken the words aloud before. One psychotherapist says, "The first time I really let in that safety and support, I heard myself say, 'I want to speak more openly about the spirituality in my work. I've been disguising it on purpose so as not to offend anyone. I want to speak with the enthusiasm and joy for spirituality that I have.' That changed my work completely. Now I do speak about spirituality in my work, and it has transformed at the energy level where all movement begins."

Witnessing one another: healing through shared vulnerability

Part of healing the Inner Speaker is witnessing other people healing their Inner Speakers. We are part of their healing, and they are part of ours. The healing is synergistic; the whole becomes greater than the sum of the parts.

As each person becomes vulnerable in front of the room, and stretches to take in the support, it gets easier for everyone to open up. The room gets safer and safer. We see years of holding on fall away for other people, and we know that our support is helping to make that possible. We all move through our fears, both in front of the room and as we sit in the audience.

"You're never up there alone," says Marty Barclay, a Berkeley gardener who has become a public speaker. "We sometimes feel we're going through life alone, but Speaking Circles are a good example of life being a 'field experience.' We're all part of one field of thought, life, and energy. In Circles, we are being witnessed as works of art. That doesn't happen in too many places. Each time I witness someone moving more into himself or herself, I move more into myself."

One therapist pointed out, "A lot of the shame we experience as children is not just about a parent saying, 'Bad boy!' It's about them saying something like that *in front of other people.* One reason the Circles are so healing is that now we're not only getting positive feedback for being ourselves, but that *positive feedback is also being witnessed by other people.* Somehow we need that public aspect of healing to undo the earlier shame."

Different and the same

One of the most healing things we can experience is our common humanity with other people. Speaking Circles reveal both that we are all absolutely unique individuals, and that we are all very much alike.

"Witnessing other people again and again, I experience diversity on a whole other level," says one computer consultant. "It would be impossible for me to imitate anyone out there. We are all so different. And yet it's also obvious that we are all so alike. It's one of the beautiful paradoxes of Circles."

Another participant sees Circles as "real isolation-breakers, a way of tuning into how similar we are. It's a community builder because you get unconditional support and that bonds you. Everyone is vulnerable and has to trust, so you relate to people in a fresh and spontaneous way."

The whole purpose of healing our Inner Speaker is to become the people we were meant to be, to let go of the masks and defenses we adopted to spare ourselves pain so that we can be the people we really are—not the people others wanted us to be, or who we were pretending to be.

We heal so that we can be real. That is the subject of the next chapter. ◎

Chapter 5

Being Yourself: The Key to Compelling Rapt Attention

Being our authentic selves is the most compelling thing we can do—in life, and in front of the room.

It is both the simplest thing in the world, and a fine art.

Genuine, authentic personal presence is a rare commodity in public speaking, even at the highest levels—and it doesn't always happen even in individual communications. We may think, "I'm real with my family and close friends." But even with these people we often get trapped in roles, habits, and expectations that obscure our authentic selves.

True power lies in authenticity, tapping into our own values and experiences, and making sure that what we say is what we believe. Transformational Speaking offers us a way to find and express deeper, truer parts of ourselves—both with strangers in an audience and with the people we love most.

What is "real"?

Being real means standing before people in an open, vulnerable way without roles, masks, or expectations of any kind. We connect with people just as we are in that moment, and receive their support. Our priority is to be completely present with them, and to let whatever we say come out of that relationship.

I have seen people literally stand in front of a room reading the phone book, and keep people enthralled because they come from this place.

"The best gift of Speaking Circles has been the confidence, ability, and total freedom to be exactly who I am," says singer, songwriter, and professional speaker Jana Stanfield. "No pretenses, no smoke, no mirrors. What a revelation to find that my real, human self is what audiences like best! Even my business audiences! I think it's because it frees them to be their most real, human selves."

Being real is more than telling the truth and giving people accurate information, but it doesn't necessarily mean revealing our deepest, darkest secrets. We may do both of those things, but our authenticity comes not so much from what we say, as from how we say it.

Our presence says more than our words

Who we are speaks more loudly than what we say—with business associates, in personal relationships, and in front of the room.

What we tell people may be extremely valuable, but how they feel in relationship with us determines whether or not they hear us, trust us, and act on what we say. If we are real with them, they will pay attention, believe what we say, and be inspired to do something about it. If we aren't completely present, or if we're wearing any kind of mask, they can easily dismiss or resent us.

Most of us have had the experience of taking an instant dislike to a speaker or teacher, and resisting what he or she said even though it made good sense and might even benefit us. If a speaker is cranking out a pre-packaged message but isn't really passionate about the subject, we know it. If someone is trying to sell us something to make a quota, we know it.

We may not understand all the nuances, but we know that something is wrong. Something is not as it seems, and we become wary. What we're hearing is different from what we're sensing and feeling. That dissonance makes us edgy. We want to put some distance between us and the speaker, both mentally and physically. We certainly don't want to buy what he or she is selling.

According to a Circle Speaker who makes his living as a marketing consultant, "What really sells people on anything is the authenticity of the individual. You have to tell them about the product or service, but they have to believe you and trust you. And when you're authentic, they do trust you. They can't help but want to connect with you when you can connect with them on that level."

A homemaker put it another way: "People are not as motivated by what goes on in the head as they are by what goes on in the heart."

Our message is important—but our depth of commitment to it and our relationship with the audience is even more so.

It's not the crime; it's the cover-up

Richard Nixon learned this lesson during the Watergate investigations, and it is equally true for public speaking.

What makes people uneasy is not that we are nervous or fearful; it's that *we are upset about being nervous or afraid, and trying to cover it up or make it go away.* People are usually fine if we acknowledge our nervousness. But they cringe if we pretend to be cavalier, arrogant, nonchalant, or blasé—when they can feel our unease. They know we're lying, and they'll have trouble believing anything else we say.

"When I got comfortable with my shyness, I didn't mind talking to groups," says the head of a decorating firm. "Situations that used to terrify me, like talking to a board, became pretty simple. I used to agonize and pretend to be so confident, but now I'm just myself and it works much better."

The Flow Connection

It's not uncommon for Transformational Speakers to be anxious—and at the same time completely connected with the group and compelling their rapt attention. We feel the anxiety, but we don't judge or hide it. We may even talk about it, and about why we're nervous.

Being just the way we are—even when that isn't how we think we *should* be—is being real.

The "real zone"

We all know how it feels when the person in front of the room is truly open, relaxed, authentic, and reaching out to accept our support and relate to us.

The air becomes electric. At the same time, an enormous feeling of relief settles over the room. Everyone breathes more easily, and every pair of eyes is riveted on the speaker. That person is sharing something very personal—it might be about love, or pain, or growing, or just about being more productive at work—but it touches something deep within us, resonates with what we know about life, and gives us a shared sense of what it is to be human. Our external activities and experiences may be very different, but we know the speaker understands something about us.

"When I hit the 'real zone,' I know it," says Judith Parker, a speakers agency owner. "All of a sudden, I connect with myself and the audience. It's like playing tennis, and hitting the ball exactly right on the racquet, in the sweet spot. There's no energy spent, it just flows and I feel that connection. After the first time I had that experience in the Speaking Circle, I could recreate it more consistently in front of groups of fifty or even hundreds!"

The "real zone" isn't a place where we arrive once, and then we're there and we never have to think about it again. Our authenticity is different in every moment, because every moment is different and we are different in it. We need to keep coming back to ourselves, and to our connection with other people in every moment—just as actors in a play must speak the same lines every night, but also recreate the experience anew for each audience.

"In life, we play all sorts of roles. In Speaking Circles, we have a chance to play our deepest selves," says a Circle veteran who is a mortgage broker. "We're always trying on attitudes and styles, but we don't have any place that's safe to try on being who we really are. Here, we know we can do that and not be chastised for it."

Why being real is mesmerizing

We human beings crave deep, genuine experiences of one another. These experiences are the most compelling, entertaining, enlivening, and uplifting things that can happen in our lives. They are what love, tragedy, comedy, and drama are all about. Think about the most fascinating experiences you have had. They probably involve you, and/or others, being fully, authentically human. When we are deeply and openly ourselves, people become transfixed. When we learn to do that in front of a room, we become a tremendous force for good. "We don't always bring our personhood forward in professions," says a personnel manager. "We bring our capacities, but not our vulnerabilities. It's a challenge to be present in that way out there in the world, but people's response is overwhelmingly positive when we do."

The more we open up and receive people's support, the more of ourselves we discover, the more we share with them, and the more they receive us and our message. It's an inspirational, uplifting upward cycle.

Being real is also irresistible because when we are genuinely *ourselves*, we give the audience permission to be genuinely *themselves*. If we are relaxed enough to stand in all of our greatness and vulnerability, then the audience feels comfortable with their greatness and vulnerability. Being real in front of a group holds up a mirror to the audience and lets everyone enjoy the richness of the human spirit in one another. That is not a common experience in our society, and people can't get enough of it.

"We've been taught that when you're in front of an audience, you have to perform," says a business consultant. "You have to create an image to fit what those people want. Transformational Speaking is about letting who you are come out and interact with *other* people's selves. The reason it's so powerful is that people are looking everywhere for that kind of connection in this world."

John Harrison, a San Francisco writer and former stutterer who facilitates Speaking Circles for members of the stuttering community, observes:

> Stutterers often grow up self-conscious and are usually very uncomfortable in front of an audience. Audience members immediately sense this, and because they pick up on the speaker's feelings, they become uncomfortable themselves.
>
> I point out that film directors play upon the audience's quickness to react to what others are feeling. For example, when someone pulls a gun on the hero, the director generally cuts to a reaction shot. Is the hero reacting fearfully? Then the audience will worry. On the other hand, if the hero is acting nonchalant, then the audience figures that the situation is under control, and they relax.
>
> I tell people that you don't have to be fluent or perfect or put up a facade. Just show up as who you are. Show up as real. If you're having trouble speaking, be up front about it. If you're feeling scared, allow the fear to be there, perhaps even acknowledge it. When the audience realizes that you're choosing to accept your experience, and that you're willing to reveal your genuine self, they're much more likely to settle back and connect with you and what you have to say. By accepting and projecting your own humanity, you're also making it okay for *them* to be real, to be *themselves*. When people put their real selves forward, they often are mesmerizing, even though they may not be fluent.

Fluency is usually an outgrowth, though not the emphasis, of Speaking Circles. The emphasis is on being real and becoming comfortable with ourselves, which causes our audiences to lean back and luxuriate in this rare permission to be comfortable with themselves.

What being real is NOT

Being real should be as natural as the sun rising and the grass growing, but often the training we receive as speakers actually keeps us from being authentic, and acts as a camouflage for our real selves.

This professional training usually includes such performance techniques as stylized gestures, carefully planned movements on the stage, a practiced voice tone for every sentence, strategized "meaningful" pauses, and knowing exactly when we will slow down or speed up our speech. All these techniques are attempts to create substance or meaning through style—and it just can't be done that way.

Many speaking programs give lip service to speaking authentically, but what they actually teach is technology and mechanics. It's as if they were using a book of techniques on how to do "relationship" that prescribed certain words and behaviors to produce specific results. On the first date, for instance, your instruction might be to go to a Chinese restaurant and a movie. When you proposed, the stage direction might be to kneel down on your right knee and pause for three seconds before speaking. That's not how real relationships work, and it's not how effective speaking works.

In fact, people who start out with coaching that makes them look "polished" from day one often miss the chance to let their own natural style emerge. They have it all planned out and practiced, instead of seeing what kind of gestures, footwork, and voice tone evolve organically out of their own enthusiasm, personality, and content.

When we've used those performance techniques for a long time and they have brought us some success, we may feel too vulnerable to let go of them.

Says Jane Bell, a Speaking Circle facilitator:

> I was a skilled public speaker. I knew how to stand up and entertain, and I was very comfortable with the traditional way. Transformational Speaking was profound for me because I had to go through a process of stripping away

a facade. When I began to show up as a more real and authentic speaker, it impacted every area of my life and all my relationships. I was more present, more genuine, and more vulnerable. I let people see me more, so I got more love, more trust, and more community.

This process lets us see how beautiful people really are, and we realize we don't need all those masks we've developed to hide our fear or pain.

The head of a public relations firm says,

Letting go of the techniques meant that I was just there, in my innermost being. We don't do that much in this world, and we might think, "Well, that leaves me very vulnerable." I don't think it does. By opening myself up, it doesn't mean I'm totally defenseless or that I don't have my own boundaries. It just means I get rid of the shields or roles I might normally play. I actually felt people reaching out to me. When you open up, you're inviting people to support you. When the support comes, it invites you to open up even more.

When we go beyond "looking good" in front of the room, we open up enormous possibilities for ourselves, and for others to support us.

A magazine once asked if I could give any tips for an article on "Stage Skills." "Yes," I said. "Realize that stage skills are vastly overrated. The best thing we can do is to open our hearts, and slow down enough to enjoy ourselves and be with the individuals in our audience."

The difference between technical speaking and Transformational Speaking is the difference between following an instruction to "pause for five beats," or following a guideline to stay silent to let our words sink in as we gaze at individual people in the audience and "listen" to them get it.

Transformational Speaking asks us to stand *together* with our audience, not above them. It's speaking from the inside out, rather than from the outside in. Our insides speak to their insides, instead of our outsides speaking to their outsides.

"I never want to get caught up in the slickness," says another professional speaker. "We have to forget about being good, and remember to be ourselves."

Finding our natural style

We can't go wrong when we're ourselves, because nobody does "us" as well as we do.

Transformational Speaking encourages us to find our own individual style. That may take a little time and involve some discomfort because we don't get to wear masks, but the result is a way of being with audiences that is natural, organic, and effortless. *And* achieves astounding results.

"The great challenge, and the great reward, is just to be present," says a nurse who speaks on healing and transformational subjects. "It sounds simple, but you have to be willing to tolerate whatever discomfort comes up without jumping into performing. You just have to sit still and be in your own skin."

Sometimes people actually have their natural styles coached *out* of them. For instance, a coach might tell someone, "Don't speak so fast! Slow down!" But if this person is a Type A personality or from New York, their natural style may be fast! He may talk fast, walk fast, think fast, and look and feel strange if he is forced to be any other way. Slowing down could actually take away his power.

He might find it helpful to pause frequently so that Type B's and non-New Yorkers can catch up—and so that he himself can breathe, recapture the connection, and make sure he's still heading in the direction he wants to go. But talking fast can be very effective for him if that's his natural style.

"Finding our own voice is about being free," says one real estate developer. "When I'm up there in my truth, not doing it any certain way, just being myself, I see people sort of wake up, like they understand. I'm not speaking anyone else's speech, not doing anyone else's thing. I'm just being me, being present, coming from my heart."

Modeling our topic

Another way to be real in front of the room is to live our message, to become the embodiment and model of our topic.

If we're talking about being authentic in sales presentations, for instance, we can be authentic as we speak. If we're talking about supporting employees in being more productive, we can be the embodiment of support for our audience. If we're speaking about looking for the best in others in relationships, we can look for the best in our audience—even if they seem sleepy or uninterested.

This modeling of the topic is another paradigm shift—from *telling* people what to do, to actually *being* that behavior for them.

A director of TV commercials told me about her experience of modeling her topic.

> I had just flown into town expecting to make a presentation for five people in a little conference room, and they told me I'd be doing it for 400 potential clients in the auditorium! My knees went weak, but I just decided to be me and let the chips fall where they might. I hung out with them, told stories, talked about work, and wove everything together as I would with a friend.
>
> My subject was the power of truth and keeping our integrity, and I did that by being myself with them, and keeping my own truth and integrity. I *became* the speech, and embodied what I said. People came up afterward and said, "I didn't know it was going to be that inspirational"—and it came just from relaxing and being myself.

If we want to bring light to the world, we have to be that light. When we're real with people, they sense the light in us and feel an opening within themselves. If someone is speaking from his or her authentic passion, we can feel the truth behind every word and gesture. Our radar responds with warmth, openness, and a desire to support and connect with that person.

Being real in business

Being real isn't just a New Age concept, or some therapist's good idea. It's the wave that business leaders are riding—not only because it is good for our health and well-being, but because it produces results.

Larry Prochazka, a Colorado trainer for Fortune 500 companies, offers this advice.

Presence, realness, authenticity are qualities that evoke an audience to be authentic.

It is not the trainers' experience, their training or background, that determines who is effective—and even who is hired. It is their ability to be human and relate as a person with the individuals in the room. A formal presenter invites an audience to relate formally, which prevents people from diving into the real issues underlying current problems. A cute presenter who uses clever stories and jokes invites resentments and makes people ask, "Why don't they relate to me? Why don't they get real?"

Safety is essential for deep work to take place. A real, authentic, human being who embraces and receives an audience creates a safe environment in which to share and discuss. Deeper issues, honest issues identified at a personal level results in change.

So many different waves of training have swept through the corporate world in the past ten years, many with little impact. Companies are starting to realize that training doesn't make as much difference as the trainer does. People can read trainers. They can tell who they are, what they stand for, what their character is, whether they trust them to work with their people. It is an old cliché, but it's true..."It's you they hire." Develop more of the human being, bring more to the table, and watch training effectiveness improve.

How do we get to "real"?

We can't "try" to be real. We can just relax and let ourselves be
wherever we are—calm, hopeful, nervous, shut down, ecstatic, sad,
focused, joyful, quiet, angry, or blissful. When we relax, remember that we already *are* ourselves, and settle down into genuine,
supportive connections with other people, everything starts to
come together. We can almost feel ourselves entering the "real
zone."

Speaking Circles are the perfect place to practice doing this. It
seems simplistic to say that having a group's unconditional support allows us to go within and be real, but I've been watching it
happen since 1989 and it works every time.

We all need other people to mirror back to us who we are. We
needed that as children, and we need it as adults. It's in our connection with others that we find our real selves—or experience
ourselves in a new and fuller way through their eyes.

"My goal is to come from my soul, so that I can reach the souls
of the people in the audience," says one professional speaker. "I
practice that every time in my Circle. When I am being myself,
wherever that is, people are touched. Then I can share my truth
and my inner work with them, and they get it."

Once we find where "real" is, we can start living and communicating from there more and more—in front of the room and in
life. This process reminded one Speaking Circle participant of what
his meditation teacher said about our true selves. The teacher
compared finding our authentic selves with dipping a cloth into a
vat of red dye over and over again. The first time we dip the cloth
in the dye, it emerges a brilliant red. But when we put it out in the
sun for a while, it fades. The next time we dip the cloth, it holds
the color a little longer. The next time, even longer. The teacher's
point was that if we keep immersing ourselves in experiences of
the our true selves, eventually our outsides and our insides are the
same. We don't "fade" the minute we get away from the vat of
dye.

To get to "real," we also need permission to experiment. Sometimes we have to act out all the "unreal" parts of ourselves, the

personas and masks, before we can reach deep into our truest selves. Speaking Circles give us a place to do this, to blow off steam and make "mistakes" in the company of loving, supportive people. We get all the surface cover-ups out of the way, and what emerges is our radiant, unadulterated selves.

Letting ourselves be

Giving ourselves permission to be wherever we are enriches our experience of ourselves and others in many different ways. Here are a few of the benefits that Circle Speakers have realized:

- *Relaxation.* "Whether I'm talking with friends, associates, or people I've just met, I am more real. I say what I really want to say, without being worried how I am coming across or getting emotional. Most of the time I am able to take my time, breathe, and let the words form naturally."
- *Authenticity.* "I've learned to accept my own idiosyncrasies as a speaker rather than learning a formula that fits a different personality type and mind-set. I can relax and have fun, and let my natural enthusiasm come though rather than using artificial hype."
- *Self-acceptance.* "The main thing Transformational Speaking gives me is permission to be myself, and permission to relate to the audience. I never thought you were supposed to do that. I'm a natural-born cheerleader, so I would always sit up front and soak up what the speaker was saying. I always gave speakers a lot of eye contact, but they weren't comfortable receiving it. I would think, 'You're the speaker; where am I supposed to look if not at you?' But I began to think that as a speaker, I wasn't supposed to relate or make contact with individuals. It was mind-blowing and hugely freeing to start doing that."
- *Flexibility.* "I love being able to express different emotions— vulnerable, sad, whatever. My whole childhood, I never cried in front of anyone. I would leave rather than cry, and now I've cried in front of numerous Speaking Circles because that's what came up. And I know it's a valuable—even a generous

and impactful—thing to do, to share your whole self in that way."

- *Power.* "I know that my biggest selling point is me, and I can feel the difference between trying to be someone else and being who I really am and just trusting that."

Living on-stage

The greatest joy in speaking comes when there is no difference between how we live on-stage, and how we live off-stage.

Most of us learn to get smaller and smaller when we step onto the stage. We're taught to tailor ourselves to whatever we think the audience wants. We are one way for one group, another way for another. So when we're speaking, at the time we most want to be ourselves, we often find that less and less of our real selves shows up.

The antidote to this condition is a safe environment in which to be ourselves on-stage, which is what Speaking Circles give us. We learn to let more and more of ourselves come with us to the podium, and that makes us charismatic in front of the room, in social situations, and in business. We become bigger people, and are just as much ourselves in public as we are in private.

Songwriter and singer Carly Simon once told an interviewer on "Good Morning America" that she had terrible stage fright and could never hide it because everything she's feeling shows on her face. If she's angry, frustrated, or frightened, everybody knows it. She told the interviewer that this wasn't always "appropriate," but as she was being interviewed she was extraordinarily radiant and lovely. She wasn't just giving an interview, she was living life fully, as herself. And when she sang, she wasn't just singing; she was living. There was no difference between how she was on-stage, and how she was off-stage.

Marilyn King is a former Olympic pentathlete who speaks to corporations on excellence and peak performance. Marilyn says that her biggest challenge was to believe that she could just step onto the stage, connect with people, and trust that the right words would come. Some years ago, she had a chance to try it out.

I usually use mind-maps as notes when I speak, but this particular night I just wasn't happy with what I'd put together. I redid my notes three times and still wasn't happy. On an impulse, I just tore them up and left them in a waste basket. Then I walked across the campus to the hall where I was speaking—in shock. A few minutes later I was standing behind that heavy black curtain, terrified. As I listened to my introduction, I kept bumping into a piece of furniture backstage, a tall four-legged stool.

That stool evoked a memory of something I'd envisioned, that someday I would take a tall stool out to the stage and just plop myself down on it and start talking spontaneously to an audience. The next thing I heard was, "Please welcome Marilyn King!"

I picked up the stool, and ceremoniously set it down in the middle of the stage. I said to the audience, "I've always wanted to do this!" and they burst into applause. I told them about the torn-up notes and off I went, just talking. It was great!

I always try to put some levity into my talks, but no one would mistake me for a comedienne. That night, I followed all sorts of little thoughts that occurred to me, things I would say in conversation but not on stage, and they made people laugh. Listening to the tape later, there were 42 times when people just burst into spontaneous applause or laughter, and a lot of them were from those off-the-cuff remarks. I loved it.

Transformational speaking is about bringing our lives to the stage, and taking what we get on the stage to the rest of our lives. The best and easiest way to do that is to be the people we really are, both on stage and in our lives—ourselves. ◎

Chapter 6

 **Listening with the Third Ear**

On May 27, 1994, I spent 5 minutes with my mom, the night before she died. She wasn't communicating, so all I could do was listen to her silence. In that 5 minutes, I fully heard her for the first time in my life.

My mother was a great listener. She taught me how to listen lovingly to people's silences, as well as to their words. As a speaking coach, I've learned that the key to being fully heard is to listen to your audience *even while you are speaking to them.* It's a secret that gives you tremendous power in a world where people often seem too busy or too apathetic to pay attention.

The deep listening we practice in Transformational Speaking is at the heart of effective speaking. It may also be the key ingredient in successful relationships, business skills such as management and team building, and all good communication.

What we crave

What everybody craves more than anything else is to be fully seen and fully heard, and to be accepted exactly the way they are. If we are the ones who are doing the listening and accepting, then we have what the world wants most.

In my experience, speakers rarely listen to their audiences. More often, they listen only to what is going in inside their own heads—to their own calculations, decisions, and judgments. Even before they walk to the podium, they've often decided who is sitting in front of them and what those people are like, whether the audience is composed of doctors, business people, secretaries, orchid growers, or club women. Then they speak to their own ideas about doctors, business people, secretaries, orchid growers, or club women—instead of to the individuals who are actually sitting in the audience.

These speakers rarely find out what the people in their audiences really care about, what their hopes and dreams are, what they want from the speaker's time with them, or what questions they have. They usually just deliver their script, and don't even know how people are reacting to them.

These kinds of presenters are like sound systems with huge speakers, but receivers that are too weak to pick up the signals clearly. No matter how valuable their information, or how polished their delivery, it doesn't touch the audience deeply or inspire them to action. People feel vaguely disconnected and disrespected, because they are not heard as individuals or as a group.

As Transformational Speakers, we know that people deserve our respect. We recognize that each moment is fluid, each person is unique, and that we have to keep listening all the time to people's reactions and energy flow.

We accept our audience exactly the way they are, without trying to fix them, change them, or make them better—and without dwelling on how they "should" be. They may be tired, cranky, excited, hostile, or warm and friendly. They may shift from one of these feelings to another midway through our talk, or every five minutes. They may be eating their lunches. Or talking to one another. Some of them may get up and leave. We let them be wherever they are. We may speak to a problem if it's appropriate, but we don't pretend the people in the audience are something they are not (friendly when they are cranky, or interested in us when they are tired or hungry), and we don't try to talk them out of it.

People who feel heard and accepted listen to other people. The more we listen to and accept our audience, the more they will hear us. When we give people what everybody wants more than anything else on earth, speaking feels like gliding on the wind rather than trudging up a hill.

The art of listening

We're told that enlightened people see with the third eye. Their vision goes beyond the physical plane to an intuitive level where they perceive a deeper Truth. In Transformational Speaking, we learn to listen with the third ear. We hear in a different dimension, behind the words to what people are actually sensing and feeling, and even to who they are.

Listening with the third ear is an art. It means listening to the whole person, experiencing that individual on a deep level and "receiving" his or her presence—often in ways that are non-verbal. We listen with our hearts to the other person's heart. In Transformational Speaking, "listening" and "receiving" are the same thing. We don't put up walls between us and them, even if they are not thinking or feeling what we want them to think and feel. We stay open to them, and go with the ebb and flow of our relationship.

As we look out into the audience, we see the extraordinary beauty of each person, and the light within each individual. The beauty we see out there is reflected in our own eyes, and that is what makes Transformational Speakers so irresistible. People see their own best nature mirrored in us.

This is not merely the "active listening" taught in communications courses, which consists of techniques like asking the right questions, mirroring body language, and paraphrasing back to the person what you are hearing. The listening of Transformational Speaking is a heart connection, a new dimension of hearing that honors people and makes them feel fully heard, without any demand for them to perform or to be any particular way.

This kind of listening takes place at the level of our souls. It is a fluid process that can't be codified into a list of action steps or "to do"s. It is a place we come from, rather than an action we take.

Most of us have done this kind of listening in close personal relationships. We sense where the other person is, even when no words are exchanged. We can feel their anger, love, sadness, frustration, elation, confusion, or concern. If we love them, we let them be there. We don't withdraw from them, even when we are put off or afraid. We stay in the connection, in the relationship, whether it's ecstatic or uncomfortable. We hear what they say, and we also appreciate how precious a silence can be.

As Transformational Speakers, we bring this same openness and sensitivity into our relationships with casual friends, business associates, customers, clients, and a room full of people. We receive their presence and support—whether they are sitting in the audience, having breakfast with us, hashing through a difficult business deal, or about to put us way over the top of a sales quota.

Transformational listening can't be *taught*, but it can be *caught* by watching people do it and practicing it in Speaking Circles.

San Francisco mortgage broker Judy Shaper says:

> When we listen for the positive, as we do in Circles, we start listening to *everyone* with a different ear. Tich Nhat Hanh, a contemporary Buddhist teacher, uses seeds as a metaphor for consciousness. If we water the seeds of joy and happiness, our living room will be so full of grace that when the seeds of negativity sprout, there will be little room for them to flourish. Speaking Circle listening gives us experience in watering the seeds of positive living. I always leave a Circle feeling happier and closer to my true spirit. I experience more comfort just being in the world.

"Listening Circles"

Many people feel that they get at least as much value from listening as they do from speaking in Circles, and think they should be called "Listening Circles" because both the speaker and the audience give top priority to listening.

One participant tells of watching a woman stand on the riser in silence for her entire 5 minutes, just going from one person to the next, listening to them and receiving each person's presence without any words. "She had such deep listening and open acceptance. There was incredible bonding. I felt I knew her in ways that probably couldn't have come if she'd spent the whole time talking."

Our job in Circles is to put aside the small, defensive parts of ourselves and simply be with people in a nonjudgmental, noncritical, accepting, and loving way. The good feelings we experience from doing this are intense and immediate. That makes it easier to practice this state when we go back into the world. One participant described it this way: "Listening forces me to go to a higher self. If I'm feeling judgmental, sometimes I have to go to a different frequency to find something that's both honest and positive. I have to stretch at first, but then it's so much fun to see the good rather than be critical, I get so involved I forget when it's going to be my turn. Then, I can take that higher listening and higher self back out into my life and business."

Another said, "What I get from that kind of listening is peace of mind. Just sitting back and letting go of judgment and expectation, luxuriating in really accepting that person and being able to feel good about whatever he or she does, is tremendously relaxing."

When people first start coming to Circles, they often tell me their goals are to think better on their feet, to relax more in front of groups, to be more dynamic, or to find or clarify their message. These results usually occur—but when we're actually in front of the room, *we only have control over one thing.* The only thing we can control is *how much we receive, or listen to, our audience.* How much can we let them in? How much can we look out there and see the beauty and wonder of each person?

That is our primary practice in Speaking/Listening Circles, whether we are in the audience or in front of the group—and that is why Transformational Speakers are so powerful, not just on the platform, but in business and in relationships of all kinds.

Listen BEFORE you speak

Most of us lived for years with a wounded Inner Speaker, and even experienced Transformational Speakers may have some residual anxiety when we get up to speak. Usually, our fear is that the audience will sit in judgment of us. We forget that most people are sitting out there just hoping we don't embarrass ourselves as much as they're afraid *they* would embarrass themselves if they were in our shoes—and looking at us with at least some degree of support and goodwill.

That support is there for us to accept—or not. If a speaker doesn't pause to take it in before he speaks, but instead dives headlong into his script or into amenities like "Hiya, folks! How's everybody? It's great to be here!" he is putting up a hand to the group and saying, "No, thank you. I don't need your support. I can do this myself."

This separates him from the audience and severely limits the rapport that he can establish with them—even if he does everything else right. The first thing he has said to the group is "Stay away! Don't connect with me."

Yet his words probably say something different from this, so the first thing he shows the audience is that they can't believe him. He isn't intentionally lying, but they know he's not authentic. They may also suspect that he doesn't respect them, in which case they may resent him. He has denied that he is vulnerable, which makes it impossible for *them* to be vulnerable. The relationship has started off with the wrong dynamic, and he will be working the rest of the time to "bring them along."

If, on the other hand, we stand for at least one deep breath and take in that support before we start to speak, we have a relationship with those people before we even open our mouths—whether we are speaking in a boardroom, a church sanctuary, or over coffee.

At first it can be uncomfortable to stand in the silence and receive their support, rather than filling that void with our own words and energy. But if we fill up the space, there is no room for them. We have to give them a chance to come to us. When we let in their goodwill, we begin the relationship on equal footing. We are all human beings together, we all need support, and we can all reach out to one another.

In that time of silence, we receive into our hearts the full support of the audience. We experience being the center of attention with no need to perform. We let people see our beauty, and we see theirs. We make soft eye contact with one individual, then another, then another. We don't look at "the group"; we look at individual people and make a connection. We look to their higher selves and enjoy basking in that mutual regard. When we connect with people on this heart level, a current is sparked that is electric. We feel the contact, and get energized as the rapport washes through us.

Performance anxiety dissolves as we focus on these people, feel them, and breathe them in. We actually take a deep breath and imagine breathing in their support. The temptation to rush our words or our thoughts drops away. We stand patiently within this soulful connection.

This silent moment may last a few seconds, or a few minutes. We usually let it be at least 5 to 10 seconds. (In Speaking Circles, people so relish this wonderful feeling of connection that they sometimes prefer to stand silently for their entire 3-minute check-in.)

The three B's help us open up to our audience and explore their support:

1. *Be still.*
2. *Be silent.*
3. *Be receptive.*

One speaker tells how she stays open to the support: "The keys for me are remembering that the audience *wants* to hear what I have to say, and *wants* to be included. That makes it so much easier."

This process shatters the myth that to be compelling, speakers must *give* to their audiences, that the audience's reaction to them is based on the quality of what they put forward. It is our *receptivity* that draws people to us. It is what we let them give us, rather than what we give to them. People love to have their gifts received. As we take in their support, we use it to energize our presence and our message, and send it back to them multiplied many times over. That is what makes them listen to and receive us.

"There's an outrageous stream of energy available from being the focus of a group's attention. When I let it in and speak within that stream, magic happens. I speak from my heart into their hearts," says one minister who is a Transformational Speaker.

The more deeply we listen to others, the better we can hear ourselves. Pausing before we speak to listen to our audience also gets us centered before we begin talking.

Listen WHILE you speak

Pausing silently to receive the audience's support before we speak creates a sacred ground for our talk. To keep that field of resonance with our audience, we have to keep listening to them. The more we keep noticing and receiving our audience as we speak, the more they will hear us.

In Speaking Circles, we resist the urge to think, "Now they've given to me, so I have to give to them." Our socialization tells us it's selfish or narcissistic to keep receiving, but it's by receiving from the group that we give to them. We give to them with our presence as well as with our information, but this happens *because* we remember to keep taking in their support and listening to where they are. It's natural for energy to move from our audience, the many—to us, the one.

We remember to slow down, and take in one person's support at a time. We move toward them and honor them, rather than distancing ourselves from them or trying to dominate them. We may pause as we speak—not "a pregnant pause" for effect, but to "hear" the support, take nourishment from it, let it build, and feed it back to the audience as passion. We listen to them listening to us, and the energy keeps building.

"That circle of constant feedback is like reading and being read by the audience," says an attorney. "When I'm really on, that's what happening. I have a challenge in this area because I tend to be in my head, and it's the best feeling in the world to relax into my heart."

"I didn't get this part at first," says a software sales person, "but I just practiced doing it anyway. Now I see that the audience speaks to us all the time and quite often we aren't listening."

Listening to the audience as we speak also tells us if they are hearing everything we say, or if we need to slow down so that they can take in more. Kevin Davis, sales trainer and author of *Getting Into Your Customer's Head* (Random House, 1996), notes that most sales people have perfected a conventional 4-step selling process—but studies show that today's customer is using an 8-step buying process. *So most salespeople sell faster than customers are willing to buy.* His conclusion is, "Sell slower to sell more."

Speakers sometimes do the same thing. We talk faster than the audience can listen, and impart more information than they can absorb. We may need to slow down to be heard better. Davis says, "Speaking Circles are a way to practice slowing down and expanding one's presence, and effectiveness, with groups."

When we're listening, we know exactly when and how to slow down.

Listen AFTER you speak

When we're finished speaking, we stand in front of the group and take in the applause they give us. We don't run down from the platform with a sideways wave, or refuse to make eye contact, or roll our eyes in mock denial that we were any good. We stand before them, open and receptive, taking in their appreciation and applause.

The first time people come to Speaking Circles, I almost always have to send them back to the platform to listen to the audience's applause when they are finished speaking—because brushing off compliments and resisting praise is "good manners." But think about how this feels when you are sitting in the audience, trying to tell the speaker you appreciate them. It's no fun to be rebuffed. One person in a Circle of professional speakers said, "The applause is just like a hug, and we should be able to accept a well-intentioned hug."

Often the "window/mirror" notion helps people listen to the audience before, during, and after they speak.

Turn your mirror into a window

Many speakers act as if they have a mirror between them and the audience. They can never really see the people sitting in front of them, because the mirror only reflects back their own image. All their attention is on themselves. No wonder they are self-conscious, and try to cover it up with masks or styles.

The trick to listening to the audience before, during, and after we speak is to *turn that mirror into a window*. We let them see us, and put our attention on them. The connection is sparked, and all of us are energized again.

Turning the mirror into a window also works wonders to reduce stage fright and performance anxiety. If all we have to stare at is a mirror, it's almost impossible not to wonder if we're doing everything right, if we're giving enough, and if we're avoiding all the mistakes that make up our worst nightmares. When all we can see is ourselves, the inner critic goes wild. Putting our attention on the other side of the window relaxes us and gives us something else to think about.

A child counselor who speaks to national audiences says, "Before, I was so focused on where *I* was that I couldn't see where *they* were. This work gave me the confidence to just get up there and freewheel. I'd never done that before. The fear dissipated."

"Focusing on what's happening in our relationship together made me relax about how I was doing," says a marketing representative. "Those people weren't just a blur, a mass of people rather than individuals. Before, I was afraid of what they must think of me. When I just notice what they're about, it takes the pressure off."

Receiving our audience through a window, rather than blocking them out with a mirror, lets them be part of the relationship. We start to see that receiving is really the same as giving. There is no distinction between the energy coming in and the energy going out. It's just connection. We start to trust the relationship and move within its flow, like playing among the rainbows from a crystal in sunlight.

"The best part is that give and take with the audience," says a financial consultant. "We do the talk together, as if we're one. Their emotion, my emotion; their insight, my insight. It's a kind of breathing together, sighing together, trembling together, grinning together. It feels like a circle of emotion, acceptance, intimacy, and magic. It's a circle of energy coming from them to me, to them, to me. I can see them through love instead of fear. They actually *become* the best way I see them."

Ann Weiser Cornell, author of *The Power of Focusing: A Practical Guide to Emotional Self-Healing* (New Harbinger, 1996) and teacher of the Focusing Technique, tells of a breakthrough in listening.

> As the incoming President of the Association of Humanistic Psychology, I was expected to give a fund-raising talk at the annual conference, to an audience of more than 500. I was dreading it. My strategy for surviving public speaking situations in the past had been to write the talk word-for-word and then memorize it so thoroughly that I could deliver it as if it weren't memorized. If I didn't do that, I felt

awkward and self-critical, and afterward could only remember how many times I'd said "um" and "ah."

I heard about Transformational Speaking and joined a Circle. I began enjoying myself immediately. I felt safe and confident as my ability to connect with an audience in the moment grew. I also felt excited because I could tell that this new approach had something special.

What especially impressed me was the impact I felt as I watched the others. They were just being present, being real, receiving the energy of the audience. And yet they were spellbinding!

My only doubt was whether the magic of our intimate Speaking Circle would translate to an auditorium of 500 people. But I was willing to try.

When I gave my fund-raising talk, I stood and received the audience before I said anything, because I had learned that people need to be received before they can hear you. I started with a simple personal story that had meaning for me. I breathed, connected with people, talked to one person at a time, waited until they got it before I moved on, and said everything out of my connection with people, instead of from notes.

That was the most satisfying fund-raising talk we had had in years. We received double the amount we had been expecting. And people came up to me afterward and said, "I don't know what it is, but when you're up on stage, I relax."

Today I give talks frequently and I bless Speaking Circles every time I do. Speaking in front of groups is now one of the greatest pleasures of my life. There is a flow of energy that seems to come into me from the group, which then flows back through me to them. We all get high and have a great time! I feel as though my natural gifts as a communicator have been unblocked—and I'm convinced that all people have these gifts.

More power to Transformational Speaking!

Listening is charismatic

Most people assume that charisma is a kind of sparkling confidence that only certain people can radiate. I believe charisma isn't something we *project*, but a way we *listen*.

When we receive other people's energy and support, we can't help but see the beauty of their essence. That makes us attractive—in the same way that a mother's face is beautiful when she looks lovingly at her baby. Whatever we see in others is reflected on our face. This kind of charisma can belong to almost anyone, and it can be rekindled at will.

Onc Circle Speaker says:

> I was surprised to realize that I was actually somewhat dynamic, when all I was doing was receiving! I used to think that no one really wanted to listen to me, that I was boring. After the Circles, I could see that speaking was a way to share my gifts and that people could not only listen but enjoy! Listening and receiving have been my keys to being "real" as well as elegant in public.
>
> I recently did a training for professional salespeople and was the last on the panel to speak. When I stood up, I began to pour out information as everyone else had done—but it felt very mechanical. I stopped about 2 minutes into it, connected with the audience, put down my notes. I just received their presence and spoke from my heart. They said I was "captivating." When I started over, it was like settling into a place of comfort and ease.

President John F. Kennedy was a master of this art. At his press conferences, he listened to people, was wholly present to what they said, and allowed us to share in his relationship with them. On the surface, it looked as if he was giving something out—but he was actually taking in the group's goodwill, fondness, and respect. In films of his speeches, you can see him pausing graciously to let the crowd's love wash over him. That's the kind of charisma that is available to all of us.

Good listeners are good speakers

Being good listeners makes us better speakers for three reasons.

First, listening is charismatic. Charisma is a by-product of being able to receive energy and support in focused ways. The more powerful "receivers" we are, the more charismatic we become.

Second, listening teaches us about connection, about speakers, and about audiences. In the audience, we learn what makes or breaks the relationship between speaker and audience. We learn what speakers can do to strengthen or weaken that relationship. And we learn that audiences really do want to support us when we speak. We know that we sincerely support other people when they step to the podium, and so it's natural to believe that others are supporting us when we are up there.

The president of a software company says,

> I learned as a listener that it's okay to slow down at times when I'm speaking. I used to worry about being boring if I did that, but sometimes in the audience I need time to process what people say and it's better if they slow down so I can do that. I've also learned that when audiences are quiet, it doesn't necessarily mean they're bored. When I'm in the audience and really listening, my silence can indicate that I'm interested, or that I'm processing information, or even that I'm applying the message.

Third, in the audience of Speaking Circles we develop the habit of looking at other people as works of art. We take that habit with us when we speak, and when we interact with others in business and in our personal lives. At the very least, we treat ourselves and others with what professional speaker, monologist, and my friend David Roche, founder of the Church of 80% Sincerity, calls Good-Natured Tolerance.

I've often thought that there should be a Church of Good-Natured Tolerance in which our ideal was to apply Good-Natured Tolerance to all our speaking and thinking about ourselves and others. That's what actually defines the humor and uplift of Speaking Circles, and Circles would be the ritual of choice in the Church of Good-Natured Tolerance. When we feel danger and fear, we act and speak with intolerance. When we feel safe and supported, heard and seen, it's natural to apply Good-Natured Tolerance.

Practice listening with the Third Ear

We don't have to be sitting in a Speaking Circle to practice listening with the third ear. We can practice it every day, at home and at work.

If a potential customer voices an objection like, "My cash flow is just too low," we can resist the urge to jump in immediately to set the record straight, or talk them out of their point of view. Instead, we can let a silence fall. We can show them that we hear what they are saying, and that we see them as real human beings who need time to work out a challenge. When we listen to people on this deeper level, they usually tell us what they really need so that we can serve them. (We'll talk more about this kind of "Explosive Listening" in Chapter 12.)

When we talk with loved ones, particularly about uncomfortable subjects, we can let them have their say before we jump in with our good ideas. If they pause for breath, we can give them a chance to start again before leaping into the void and giving our perspective. When they feel heard by us, they will feel safe to speak from a place of deeper truth.

Many Circle Speakers have started variations on Circles for their families or work groups. Before beginning a meal or meeting, for instance, they might give each family member 2 minutes of support and positive attention while that person shares anything he or she has to say. Children love it!

Listening to life

The best thing that listening teaches us is how valuable and precious every human being is—and part of that is seeing our own value and listening to our own deeper voices.

"Deep listening has affected the way I see the world, and every relationship I have," says a teacher. "I'm not just more present and receptive, I'm more empathetic. I have a greater respect for my own foibles and growth, too."

Speaking Circle facilitator Cathy Dana uses her listening skills in her work as a hypnotherapist, and also in her personal life.

> My son Max is 4, and I discovered through Speaking Circles that my role as his mother is guardian of his creative spirit. So I give him this kind of listening and attention. My husband and I use it, too. When we have something to discuss, we give each other 5 minutes of complete, positive attention instead of just jumping in and defending our positions. I also belong to a mothers' group that tended to get a little competitive, with everybody vying for "air time." I used to sit thinking about what I was going to say and how to be heard, but one day I came in with low energy and decided, "I'll just go and listen." I enjoyed the group much more and I found that things popped up naturally to say, and that when I talked, they all turned to me and really listened.

Cathy has a black belt in aikido, and adds, "To me, this kind of listening is like aikido. 'Ai' means harmony or love. 'Ki' is energy. 'Do' means way or technique. So aikido is a way of harmonizing energy—and so is the kind of listening we do in Circles."

Listening with our hearts broadens our world. An office manager says, "The world looks a particular way through *my* eyes, and if I listen I can also see it though *other people's* eyes. It widens my view of life. It has very broad applications—in business, with friends and associates."

In the next chapter, we'll look at the natural consequence of listening—connection with other people. ◉

Chapter 7

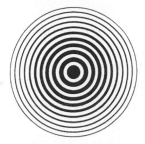

Connection is Everything

We human beings love nothing more than connecting, heart and soul, with one another. These connections inspire, energize, and give purpose to our lives and work. Most of us have experienced this synergy on a personal level. Now business leaders are discovering the power of connection, and the futility of trying to produce significant results without it.

"We are getting to the point where it is no longer enough to entertain and inform," according to futurist and professional speaker Chuck Moyer. "It is, and will be, demanded of speakers that they contribute to making a positive, permanent change in the lives of their audiences. This can only be done through honing the audience relationship skill."

Grady Jim Robinson, professional speaker and award-winning storyteller in St. Louis, wrote about "The Re-Awakening of Soul in Speaking" in his publication *The Mythmaker's Voice*.

> Your impact as a speaker lies not in something called *content* but in something called *connecting*. The game is communication—not information. Everybody has the same information, or it is easily accessible.
>
> A speaker does not walk to a microphone and give a speech. The speaker ignites an event within a context of relationships. When we lose sight of the context, the ongoing process, the in-the-moment human dynamic, we are thinking in mechanistic and archaic frameworks.

Leaders can no longer simply stand in front of a room and tell people what to do. To make an impact, we need to forge strong, heartfelt relationship with people. That means we have to be authentic and human with them. We have to let them in, so they will let our message in.

This is the very essence of Transformational Speaking. We work from the inside out. Our connection with others starts at the core of our being, and touches people at the core of their beings. That's why it is so important for us to understand the dynamics of connection.

The illusion of separation

Einstein is credited with saying, "The tragedy of human nature is the illusion of separation." We are all connected in some mysterious way, and the sorrow is that we forget that.

When we remind people by gently connecting with them, the illusion of separation is broken and we all feel the light of our oneness. We are always happiest, and at our best, when we live in that light.

The purpose of Transformational Speaking is to dissolve the illusion of separation, and that's how we come to compel rapt attention every time we speak. We humans love to experience the Truth behind the illusion, the connection behind the separation. We are inclined to listen to anyone who makes us remember.

Author and Transformational Speaker Salli Rasberry puts it this way: "I'm less intimidated by the idea of being the one 'up in front' now that I've changed my approach to speaking. It's not *me* and *them*. It's *us*, and we're dancing together."

Where connection happens

Connection happens in the heart. It happens when we are connected with ourselves, and speak from our passion into the hearts of others.

One professional speaker says, "If I'm present with myself, I have less need to control the group and the outcome of the program. I'm more spontaneous if I really check in with myself, breathe, and settle into where I am. Then from my self, I make contact with my Self, the higher part of me that will be with the participants. Then I can be spontaneous and go where *they* need to go, rather than where *I* need to go. We're connected, and that's the only way I can give them anything."

When we are at home with ourselves, we give other people permission to be at home with themselves—to relax into an acceptance of exactly who they are today. "I wanted more than anything just to speak to people in the moment, peacefully, from my heart, without thinking about what I was supposed to say," says a consultant for a Fortune 500 company. "The first time I got up in front of my Circle, I somehow let myself feel that heart connection. It was amazing. I had never spoken in front of people from such a place of peace, clarity, truth, and love."

Patrick Donadio, one of the original members of the Speaking Circle at the Ohio chapter of the National Speakers Association and current President of that chapter, is a professional speaker and consultant on personal development, empowerment, and risk taking. He says, "I'd been a professional speaker and trainer for 12 years, and was getting great evaluations but not feeling as personally connected with audiences as I wanted to be. Sometimes I felt as if I were operating on autopilot. Learning to be real about my passion kicked my presentations into a whole new gear. I talk about things that really matter to me, and people feel the difference. It's intimate and exciting. I love it and I get a much bigger, more enthusiastic response by making that connection."

That original Ohio Speaking Circle, consisting of eight professional speakers, has met regularly for two years and has sparked several other Circles in the Midwest.

Each connection is unique

Connections among people are like snowflakes: each one is unique. We all have a special way of being with one another that is different from our connection with any other person, and different from our connection with that one person at any other moment in time.

One woman said, "I could get up here for 5 minutes and not say anything at all, and someone else could get up here and not say anything at all—and it would be a completely different experience because we're two different people with two different sets of connections in two different times. That means I can't compete with anyone here, because I can't be like anyone here. *I can only get more like me."*

If we remember our own uniqueness, the uniqueness of each connection, and the need to recreate those connections minute to minute, we will never lack for intimacy with loved ones or audiences.

Instant rapport: four basic steps to connecting with any audience

Intimacy is a "be," not a "do"—but here are four basic "do's" that can dramatically enhance your "be."

1. Stand with your feet planted into the center of the earth, and listen to your audience before you begin speaking.

Take at least 5 to 10 seconds of silence so you can "arrive" before you start speaking, and to open the door to connection with your audience. Receive their support. If you really let yourself see their beauty, it will reflect back to them in your eyes.

Try standing still, even if it is uncomfortable at first. Standing still gives the group a focus: you. Standing still also prevents you from using movement as a nervous cover-up. You shouldn't feel as if you're frozen stiff—but if you absolutely can't begin your talk standing still, then movement may be a cover-up.

You will notice an elegance and sufficiency in standing still.

You may find yourself "moving out" toward people without actually moving your body. Later, when you've mastered standing still, you will find your own "dance" and organic, natural movements on the platform.

These moments of "listening" to your audience, which we discussed in the last chapter, are where you find your connection with them.

2. Speak clearly, from the heart, in short sentences.

Once you've established the connection by standing and receiving your audience in silence, keep it going by speaking in a way that makes it easy for them to receive you.

Tell a true personal story that relives an anxiety, a challenge, or an inspiring moment—that in some way makes you vulnerable. Your story can be about a dream (or nightmare) you woke up with this morning, an adventure you had trying to get there on time, or perhaps a dramatic turning point in your life or a time you felt like a failure.

Let them know that you are a human being, just as they are. You're not hiding your fears from them, and so they don't have to hide their fears from you. Give your story even more power by telling them what you learned from the event and linking it to why you are here today. (We'll talk more about your opening story in Chapter 15.)

When you speak from your heart, people know it. Last year I was invited to speak to a group of travel agency executives, but they gave me the wrong directions and I arrived an hour late—at 7:30 for a 7:30 speech. Normally, I like to get there in time to chat with people and find out something about the group.

But that night I arrived breathless and had to start speaking soon after I walked in the door. Instead of getting stressed, I just stood for a long time and received their support. When I felt the connection, I told them I'd wanted to arrive at 6:30 to find out more about them and about the travel agent business, but had gotten lost. They laughed with me. Then I just looked at them and asked, "Who *are* you!?" Again, they laughed because I clearly didn't have a clue, and was admitting it. And they paid rapt attention to me because they could tell the question was sincere. The talk flowed from there.

People would rather hear the truth than anything else we can tell them, and they can receive any message better if we speak clearly from our hearts. Whether we are presenting a budget or telling the kids to be home by ten, the words don't matter as much as our attitude. If we connect with the kids in a respectful way and let them know clearly why we want them home by ten, they're more likely to get the message. Presenting the budget may not include any deep emotional sharing, but it's bound to be more pleasant for all concerned if we are real and human, and if we connect with people as we give them the numbers. It can't hurt, and it may be very helpful.

3. Say every sentence into the eyes and heart of a human being in the audience.

Many traditional presenters speak to "the group" rather than to individuals. Their eyes sweep the audience or focus on the back wall, but they do not engage real human beings. Their eye contact is superficial, usually for only one or two seconds ("eye service," I call it), so that they take in everyone but see no one. Sometimes they seem to glaze over.

Remember that you are speaking to human beings, not just to "audience members." Each time you meet someone's eyes, speak into that person's heart. Open yourself to how it feels to be there with that person. Let him or her know how it feels to be there with you.

The first person with whom we need to connect, of course, is ourselves. If we don't feel particularly present or "here," we can take a few deep breaths to move toward our center, while we remember that connection is our first priority.

"It's connection with myself during the talk, and a deep connection with the audience, that makes it work," says one workshop leader. "By speaking to individuals, not to the whole room or crowd, I find the support and intimacy that makes it possible to relax, and to be dynamic and vulnerable at the same time."

Magic happens when we speak from our connection with individuals.

4. Spend 5 to 10 seconds of quality time with each listener before moving on to another.

The conventional speaker's practice is to make eye contact with as many people as possible for 1 to 2 seconds each. The larger the audience, the more these speakers fragment their energy. They feel pressure to scan and move, sweep and hurry—and often scuttle around the stage in the process. This approach tends to be distracting, disconnecting, and stressful both for the speaker and for the audience.

For eye contact to have impact, it needs to be at a deeper level. As Transformational Speakers, we stand still and engage individuals for up to ten seconds or so, listening to each person, making a point, and staying long enough to make sure the person has heard what we said. *The ideal is to engage each person 100%, not to contact 100% of the people.*

At first, some speakers are afraid that by engaging individuals for that long, they will exclude the rest of the audience. Just the opposite is true. Listeners feel more fully included and connected with us when we make *deeper* connections, even if we make *fewer* of them. The group values quality of connection more than quantity of contacts, so there is no need to "cover" everyone in the audience.

It's as if those people with whom we connect deeply are surrogates for the entire audience. Everyone else watches the connection and participates in it, even when our eyes are not on them. We are creating more than a connection between ourselves and that one person; we are connecting the whole audience with one another and creating a community that includes all of us.

A corporate trainer finds,

> Learning to speak to one person at a time was a breakthrough. Although I knew this and thought I practiced it, I learned in my first Circle that I didn't always do that. I saw myself not doing it on the video. I was a scanner. The day after this Circle, I presented an all-day seminar to 60 people.

Speaking in this new way created a bond I'd never had with an audience before, and it's been there ever since. I used to present *to* people, and now I feel as if I'm talking *with* them. There's much less anxiety because I'm just going to talk to people. I can just hang out with somebody, finishing a complete thought, and that builds a relationship with the whole audience.

These four basic steps to instant rapport are just as powerful at home and at work as they are in front of a room.

The power of soft eyes

When we look at individuals in the audience, we don't stare them down, "drill" them with our gaze, or make our eyes into high-beam headlights blazing out energy that demands to be returned.

Instead, we maintain a soft focus around the eyes of people in the audience. It begins the moment we step to the front of the room, and continues the whole time we are speaking. When we are present with them and "listen" to them with our "soft eyes," they feel seen and heard, safe and secure, recognized and respected. Some would say that we seek out each person's soul, and feel their attention and support pour out toward us.

Many people experience these connections happening in slow motion. Baseball players report that when they're on a hitting streak, the ball looms up to the plate huge, slow, and easy to hit—but when they're in a slump, the ball whizzes by the size of an aspirin tablet. When we keep receiving the eyes of the audience, they become big and attentive and giving. We naturally start to breath with the audience. Everyone slows down and relaxes into the connection.

Some of us are uncomfortable at first with sustained eye contact, and with good reason. Our early experience with eye contact is often related to "power tripping". Adults were trying to exert their influence over us in some way, often by telling us who we should be or denying who we were. We came to think of eye contact as a dangerous thing. It was!

In Speaking Circles, we have a safe place to learn to relax our eyes again. We look out into the audience and receive total support. We remember how that feels, and learn to enjoy and expect it. We practice it in Circles until it becomes second nature to open into "soft eyes" in front of any group.

"Riding the beams"

John W. Travis, M.D., is a Transformational Speaker who wrote about "soft eyes" in an article called "Riding the Beams," which we excerpt here.

> I avoided real eye contact until I was 52 years old. Now I'm hooked on it.
>
> In my family there was little contact, eyes or otherwise. I learned to live in my head because it was the safest place in the house.
>
> Out in the world, I learned to fake enough eye contact to pass, but it ranged from uncomfortable to terrifying. In the hundreds of talks, presentations, and workshops I gave, I scanned the audience and occasionally someone would catch my eye and I'd feel good, but mostly there was no eye contact.
>
> My medical career turned to prevention and I started the first wellness center in the world. This work eventually led me to discovering the importance of the deep bonding that occurs in so-called primitive societies who suckle, carry, and sleep with their babies. The destruction of this bond by western culture leads to autonomy, the flip side of which is estrangement and alienation.
>
> I believe eye contact is an extension of the in-arms phase that we have lost, and that the eye contact of bonded people is far more intimate than most of us experience. Through Speaking Circles I have found a new kind of eye contact in which I am fully seen and heard by other people. It's like riding on beams of energy that I had always experienced as fearsome rays from which I had to protect myself.

In Circles, we learn to ride the beams in a way that feels exalting to both speaker and audience.

A network marketer specializing in recruiting leaders says,

> I was in the habit of just scanning the audience with my eyes, moving quickly from person to person and trying to cover the whole room, but this practice of soft eye contact with one person at a time has slowed me down. I remember that these are real people and share things off the cuff I wouldn't have shared before in public. I've started doing that in my work and trainings, and have found that authenticity gives me a lot more rapport with my audiences— and more reaction from them. It's completely revolutionized how I speak.

David Bradwell, an economist and expert witness in Santa Rosa, California, and a Circle Speaker, agrees.

> I make eye contact with individual jury members before responding to each question. Developing this real, human contact with even two or three jurors is all it takes to get the whole jury listening to what I say. These people have often been hearing testimony for several weeks and as a result have gotten pretty punchy by the time I take the stand, so making that eye contact is really worthwhile if I want to be understood. I give that same attention and "listening with the eyes" to cross-examining attorneys. They try all sorts of tactics to unsettle a witness hostile to their position: anger, sarcasm, entrapment games, etc. By not rising to that bait, and by continuing to keep contact with them, I cut through the games and dramatically reduce the time they spend trying to trip me up. Even though the courtroom is a formal, adversarial setting, people still hunger for quality communication.

The electric connection

Connection is like an electric current—whether it happens between two people, or between a speaker and an audience.

Some people mistakenly think we have to be generating the electricity before we dare connect with another, but just the opposite is true. The electricity comes *after* we open to them. It doesn't *cause* the connection; it happens *out of* the connection between us. The more deeply we connect, the more electricity flows back and forth between us and the audience.

There are two ways to create more electricity in any connection. One is to increase the voltage, to pump out more energy to the audience. The other is to *decrease resistance*. In Transformational Speaking, we decrease our resistance to receiving the audience's support. We let more and more of their energy into our connection. We receive that support and send it back to them, so that the wire between us gets wider and wider, and our connection becomes deeper and deeper.

We actually widen our perspective. The "wire" gets bigger and bigger until it's as wide as the room, and can even grow until we feel it's as wide as the whole world. We are tuned into everything on the planet, and what we are saying has global implications. Sometimes when I listen to a speaker, I have the feeling that the room in which I'm sitting is the most important place in the world to be at that moment. The speaker seems to be talking about more than his or her subject; rather, about something that's very important to the world. These are the speakers who have learned to "widen the wire" to global proportions.

When we're "inside the wire" with people in the audience, it can almost feel like the "music of the spheres." Each of us is there with our own unique vibration, and we're letting our vibrations come together and join in the ultimate human experience: connection. We've broken the illusion of separation.

Keep coming back

Connection doesn't happen just once, and then stay in place indefinitely. When the electricity sparks, we may think, "Ah, I have it!" But the next minute, it's gone.

When that happens, we have to reach out again and let people in. This happens over and over in the course of a talk. It's the nature of connection. Connection can only happen "here" and "now"—and "here" and "now" are different in every nanosecond.

We can never have the same connection with the audience in this moment that we had in the last moment—and people only listen with rapt attention when they keep getting glimmers of a renewed connection. Each time they feel the new connection, they think, "Oh, I'm going to hear more. I'm going to feel good. I'm not going to feel so alone. Somebody's going to be with me."

These thoughts may not be conscious, but they're there. This is *creating* intimacy, not *simulating* it. Many speakers simulate intimacy, but Transformational Speakers actually create a home to which people can keep coming back.

Connection is always a work in progress. It's like riding a bicycle; we're constantly making the correction and coming back into balance. Then we fall out of balance again, and come back again. The connection is in constant motion, being reestablished in each new moment. The keys are to stay open, be in the moment, and keep receiving the audience.

There's only one audience

There is really only one Audience. When we understand how to connect with that Audience, we don't have to reinvent the wheel each time we stand up in front of a group. That Relationship with Audience is fundamentally the same, no matter how different the people are who are sitting before us.

It is simply a matter of standing before them in a real and open way, listening to them, and receiving their support. Once we can do that with one audience, we can do it with any audience—and everything we say and do can come out of that connection spontaneously and organically.

What we say and do will look different every time, but the nature of the connection remains the same: receiving them and responding in the moment, and giving the priority to our relationship with them rather than to a script.

There is no better place to practice that give and take, that rhythm, that fluid connection, than in a Speaking Circle. When we know how it feels in a group of ten people, we know how it feels in a group of any size. We don't worry about what we're going to say, or how we're going to say it. We may know our opening story and what we want to accomplish with our talk, but we let much of it flow out of our relationship with the audience, and the chemistry between us. We can't plan everything that is going to happen, any more than we can plan what will happen in a conversation with a friend or business associate—but we know we can trust that chemistry, and our instincts about Relationship with Audience.

I once spoke to a group of 20 interior designers at their monthly luncheon meeting. They were quite involved with one another and their work, and didn't seem very interested in listening to the speaking coach standing at one end of their table—especially since lunch was served just as I stood up to talk. The meeting was being held in a fancy room decorated like a wine cellar, and much fancy wine was flowing. I could feel a chasm opening wider and wider between them and me, until I found myself sitting down—as they were—picking up my fork, and speaking to them as I would have spoken to one other person over lunch.

The energy around the table changed instantly. I had their attention. They were listening to what I said, and immediately I got them involved in the conversation and even had them go around the room, taking turns receiving one another's support as they spoke for 2 minutes about their work.

Sitting down and engaging them on a more intimate level was instinctive. It came out of what I know about Relationship with Audience. Just as I wouldn't stand talking to one person if he or she were sitting down, I knew that I had to become one of them. I had to get on their level, quite literally. I had to stop being The Speaker, and illustrate my interest in them.

When we begin to trust our Relationship with Audience, we see that every group contains all the various aspects of humanity. We can think of the group as one organism, but one that includes all the myriad ways to be human. And every group contains parts of *us*. Relationship with Audience is like a relationship with a very complex person who has many aspects to his or her personality. Seeing and being seen by that kind of person is a powerful experience, so every encounter with a group is enlivening and fascinating.

We all want to share our experience, serve, and bring our own special message to others—but what we want most, with both individuals and groups, is the richness of simply sharing one another's presence. That is the foundation of relationship—with both individuals and Audience.

Larger connection:
the community of the Circle

One of the most striking qualities of Speaking Circles is the sense of community. That's understandable, since Circles are about connection.

When people connect from their hearts and souls to share their truths, community is a natural outcome. It's a collective force of support, of shared vulnerability, and of people having the courage to stand in their own light and shine it on others.

In the process of discovering our own uniqueness, we also realize that we are very much alike. A professional speaker told me, "Transformational Speaking offers a window to some values we don't always see in our society. We share things that are interior, not mundane surface stuff, and we have empathy with one another. That broadens and deepens my world, and gives me a sense of community with other people."

Connection with other people is what human beings want more than anything. We desperately desire to shatter the illusion of separation among us, and that is what we do in Speaking Circles. One thing that makes that possible is "vibrant vulnerability," the subject of the next chapter. ◎

Chapter 8

Vibrant Vulnerability: the Real Charisma

When we let ourselves be vulnerable and embrace whatever we are feeling in the moment, we become vibrant and magnetic.

In fact, the more accessible we become, the more the audience is drawn to us and supports us. We aren't setting ourselves up as someone wiser, better, or smoother than they are. Our vulnerability allows them to show their vulnerability. We're all just human beings together, and we're enjoying it.

Hypnotherapist Marilyn Gordon, author of *Healing is Remembering Who You Are* (WiseWord):

> I'd given a lot of talks about my work and techniques, but I'd felt over-prepared, overly organized, and wanted to just speak from my heart better. I just wanted to let go and speak. Something clicked at the Speaking Circle. It was a chance just to let the words flow out of me, to see that I could really do that. It unlocked something inside me, so that my speaking is looser, more anecdotal, more charged with loving energy. It's also taken away my stage fright.

Now Marilyn has brought Speaking Circles into her own group work with clients.

Training Consultant Catherine Joseph wrote me after an all-day Speaking Circle: "I've always tried to hide my vulnerability behind technique. The chance to stand before a group and to feel and show my vulnerability was both startling and scary. And yet I came away with an entirely different vision of myself as a speaker. I simply remember the joy of feeling scared and lovingly supported by the group as I spoke."

People are always surprised at how powerful they get when they become vulnerable.

Soft power

Because we never have to convince anyone in Speaking Circles that we are "right," we learn to stand "naked" before them in our truth, to reveal ourselves, and to stay open to our connection with them without the defenses we sometimes raise with people. This is what I call "soft power."

A minister says it this way: "To preach effectively, one must be genuinely present in simple, vulnerable humanity, connecting with the vulnerability in the audience. This builds an emotional network of communication and support. We've been taught to defend ourselves against possible negative feedback and criticism, but this process heals those critical wounds and empowers everybody."

Nervous Nirvana

Imagine turning nervousness and stage fright into a transcendent state that is actually exhilarating. That's just what graphic artist and San Diego Speaking Circle facilitator Cherie Diamond did, and she called it "Nervous Nirvana."

Nervousness is just bottled-up excitement. When we're self-conscious about it and try to hide it, the nervousness just gets worse. We get a "secondary nervousness," or nervousness about being nervous, that is uncomfortable both for us and for the audience.

When we just let our nervousness be, and perhaps even talk about it, it turns back into raw energy, radiance, enthusiasm—and even ecstasy. People who've suffered from terrible stage fright all their lives can finally say, "I've gotten through it for the first time!"

It all comes back to telling the truth, to speaking from our hearts instead of from our heads. As one career consultant said,

It's kind of hard to speak when the loudest sound is my heart. I remember the first time I spoke from here [heart] instead of from up here [head]. I saw that I didn't have to be so incredibly prepared in order to be successful. Now I don't know every word I'm going to say, and if I'm nervous I just let myself be there. That ambiguity can be scary because I want to know how it's going to turn out, but the most moving thing I can tell them is where I am right *now*.

I teach people about job search and they do have to do some preparation, but ultimately they have to trust where they are coming from and their ability to be themselves in the moment.

"Nervous Nirvana"

Your magnetic self

We usually avoid being vulnerable because, for whatever reason, we're afraid we aren't *enough*. We aren't smart enough, or charming enough, or informative enough, or inspiring enough. These are old messages, probably received in childhood, that have been playing in our heads for decades even though they have no basis in fact.

When we relax and open to our audiences, we become more magnetic than we ever could have imagined. Finding this magnetic self is just a question of letting the old tapes spin out, exploring self-love and self-acceptance, and letting ourselves be vulnerable.

Saul Eisen is a Professor of Organization Development at Sonoma State University and has his own practice as a consultant. Although most of his teaching is participatory, he often has to deliver lectures or speak to non-academic groups in workshops or conferences. Saul says, "At those times, I generally wasn't very comfortable because I'm an introvert. But in Speaking Circles, I discovered that there is a part of what I am naturally—introspective and thoughtful—that really can work quite well as a speaker if I'm willing to be me while standing there in front of people. That was the breakthrough for me."

When we're willing to be ourselves, even if we don't naturally look like what we think a "speaker" should look like, we become absolutely magnetic.

The wisdom of not knowing

Exploring deeper levels of self-expression starts with *not knowing* what to say. Real creativity comes out of a void, and we can only discover our real strength when we are willing to be vulnerable. We become truly creative speakers when we can allow anything to happen in front of the room.

Life's adventure is in not knowing what's around the bend in the road. The thrill of speaking comes when we don't know exactly what we're going to say, and let our words flow from our relationship with the audience. Of course we know our subject and the basic points we want to cover, or the story we want to tell, but if our talk really comes out of our connection with the people in front of us, we can't know in advance exactly what we will say.

Not knowing can be scary. It's easy to feel as if we're two years old again and subject to being ridiculed or attacked, ignored or put down. We have to trust our relationship with the audience, and know that the right words will come.

As we practice not knowing in Speaking Circles, we see that something always happens that is better than what we could have imagined or planned. When this happens over and over, we learn to trust the process.

That's how Transformational Speakers are able to speak on the same subject again and again, and each time present a talk that is fresh, vibrant, and different from any other they've given. Perhaps half the talk comes out of relationship with the audience, and the audience is never exactly the same. Letting them in allows the talk to take its own unique direction.

"If I'm willing to be out there without having it all together and knowing every word I'm going to say, then some amazing things come up," says a city planner.

"The biggest change that Transformational Speaking made for me was the willingness to drop into not knowing on the stage," according to a public relations specialist who also teaches meditation. "It's made me trust that something will come that both I and the audience need to hear. It blows me away that I start talking and an incredibly complete talk comes out."

The wonder of natural silence

Some speakers panic if a few seconds pass in silence. The void just feels too vulnerable. They rush in, saying anything just to end the silence. Or they finish making an important point, and rush right on to the next point without giving the audience a chance to digest what they have said.

When we talk with people we love, we never work to fill in the silences. Those silences feel comfortable. They give us time to digest what people have said, to let things sink in, to think, and just to enjoy one another's company in the quiet.

It's important to let ourselves experience the vulnerability and power of natural silences for three reasons:

1. When we move from point to point without stopping to breathe, our listeners can get breathless.

They lose focus, have trouble concentrating, and may miss what we say because there isn't enough time for our words to sink in.

2. If we allow the silence, and even sustain it, we can see whether or not people are taking in what we say.

We need to know if they are *not* following what we say, so that we won't just blaze forward and leave them even farther behind.

3. When we're not sure what to say next, it's important to relax, take a deep breath, and wait in the silence until the right words come.

This is far better than rushing ahead with something that isn't right, and pushing the whole talk in the wrong direction. When people talk about "thinking on their feet," they often imagine that this will save them from those awkward silences. Just the opposite is true. Presenters who "think on their feet" are usually those who don't mind silence. It's their ability to relax into a natural silence that lets them think on their feet so well!

When we're not comfortable with silence, then much of what we say comes from fear of silence—whether we are with one other person or 1,000 people. Think of a time when you were with another person who couldn't stop talking, and who refused to let a silence fall. The chances are, you didn't feel that person was coming from the deepest place within himself.

The old speaking paradigm was about *breaking* the silence; in

Transformational Speaking, we come from the silence. We begin in a comfortable, accepting silent connection, and let everything we say come out of the relationship between us and the audience.

"When I get out of the way, my heart and mind know what to say and how to say it," says a community leader. "It's more entertaining in many ways than theater because it's not rehearsed. Something wonderful pours out of each person's heart and there it is!"

Drawing a blank

Fear of drawing a blank is a first cousin to the fear of silence—and we can use the same antidote. We can simply stop, allow ourselves to be vulnerable, and let the silence be. We can give the problem a chance to solve itself.

If we relax, the right words come. In the silence, we breathe in the group's support, stay connected with people, and resist the temptation to rush. Almost always, the audience believes our silence is intentional.

If we start to forget when giving a "real" speech, we can always walk over to our notes on the lectern. We can take a sip of water, and give ourselves some time. If we have a script, we can refer to it. (If there are things we absolutely need to remember, they can be written down and with us on the lectern.)

We can even ask the audience, "Where was I?" I've heard speakers ask this, and the audience leaps to help. We've been taught that drawing a blank is a bad thing, but this is one of many ways it can turn to our advantage.

Sometimes we draw a blank because our talk was headed in a direction that wasn't working very well, and we knew intuitively to stop. Or perhaps we had become a little automatic, and finding ourselves in the void was a chance to reach out to connect with the audience and become more creative. In any case, we are committed to "saying no line before its time."

One of my clients tells the story of attending the symphony in San Jose to hear a famous piano soloist. A few minutes into one piece, the soloist knew that something was wrong. He stopped playing and called over the conductor. After their consultation, the conductor announced, "We're gonna start this one over again." The audience loved that, and their response was thunderous. They empathized with the soloist as he passed through the ultimate fear of failure, literally stopped the music, shared it with them, and lived through the experience. Consciously or unconsciously, they realized that he'd shared with them a life lesson that went beyond good music.

Journalist Gregg Levoy, author of the forthcoming book *Callings* (Random House), tells this story about the vulnerability of drawing a blank, and what it taught him.

> I was always good at teaching and lecturing, but I wasn't confident that I could do it without my notes. That was my worst nightmare, somehow getting caught without my notes.
>
> A few years after I attended my first Speaking Circle, I was about to start my first class as a professor at the University of New Mexico. I stepped to the front of the room, opened my briefcase, and suddenly realized I'd forgotten all my notes at home. I looked up over the top of my briefcase at a class of 40 people, panicked, then flashed back to the Speaking Circle.
>
> I knew this material. I had been living it for years. I could do this if I just told them what I knew. That turned out to be one of the best classes I'd ever had and a breakthrough. I can just be there and be vulnerable, and it's still going to turn out alright. It was a life lesson as well as a speaking lesson.

When we are past our fear of drawing a blank, then drawing a blank will never again be a problem.

Vulnerability: the hero's journey

One of the most courageous things we can do is stand before a group of people we don't know, without pretenses or defenses, and allow a relationship to develop with them out of our vulnerability. That shows us more about ourselves than almost anything we could do. It is a heroic act, and people appreciate it. That's why vibrant vulnerability elicits such strong support.

Here is what some Circle Speakers have said about their hero's journey.

- "I learned as a child to hide all my mistakes and flaws, and anything I didn't know about. I didn't realize that hiding those things actually made me weaker instead of stronger, and that protecting myself in that way set me apart from people instead of making them like me."

- "I love hitting that spot at the bottom of me where there seems to be a void, but it's really like the depths of the ocean where all the nutrients are. All the good stuff bubbles up from the bottom, from the emptiness. In that emptiness is a fullness."

- "Oddly, being vulnerable gave me a sense of presence and confidence. I used to feel competitive and would want to appear to be a certain way when I spoke. Sometimes I still collapse into those defense systems when I'm flustered, but I'm more and more willing to be out there without the need to impress, arm myself against pain, or shape myself into something I'm not. Instead, I become who I am, and that makes it fun. "

In Speaking Circles, people find that vulnerability can be their greatest strength. But what can we do when we feel overwhelmed by stage fright? The next chapter contains some surefire solutions. ◎

Chapter 9

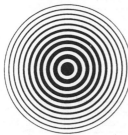

From Agony to Ecstasy: Moving through Stage Fright into Grace

Vibrant vulnerability is magnetic, but what about those times when our vulnerability seems to slip over the edge and we feel paralyzed with stage fright?

As Transformational Speakers, we can move from stage fright into grace using our basic tools of authenticity, receiving support, listening to ourselves and our audience, and connection—plus a few secrets we'll discuss in this chapter.

Stage fright is nothing more than the fear of speaking our own truth and being judged. Transformational Speaking gives us the tools to deal with that—whether the "stage" of which we're frightened is a platform, an interview, a performance evaluation, meeting the in-laws, an important presentation to a potential client, a proposal of marriage, a difficult communication to a friend, or the first day on a new job.

Our biggest fear, and where it comes from

We are a nation of people with stage fright. We've already noted that public speaking is the #1 fear among Americans, even more frightening than death. Comedian Jerry Seinfeld quotes those studies and concludes that at a funeral, most of us would rather be in the coffin than deliver the eulogy.

We also know that stage fright comes from early wounding. As children, we were either punished or made to feel embarrassed or ashamed for being ourselves, so we stopped trusting ourselves to speak and act in acceptable ways. We began editing ourselves and living in fear of making the same kind of "stupid" mistakes again— especially in public. Chapter 4 was about healing this wounded "Inner Speaker." This chapter is about what to do in those odd moments when terror sneaks back on-stage with us.

Stage fright generally shows up as fear of two rather daunting phenomena:

1. The black hole.

In the black hole, we draw a complete blank and have nothing to say. We stand, paralyzed and speechless, before an audience of three, ten, fifty, or thousands of people. Seconds drag into minutes, and still no words come. Eventually, the audience slowly gets up and leaves. That's the nightmare, the fear. *It is almost never the reality.*

I invite people in Speaking Circles to let themselves fall into the Black Hole, to stand in front of the room with nothing to say. Once they've had that experience, it rarely happens again. They survived the thing they dreaded most, so they no longer fear it. Because they don't fear it, it doesn't happen.

2. The family of 1,000.

We look out into the audience and see not co-workers, interested strangers, nice people, or potential clients, but *a room full of disapproving, reprimanding, ridiculing, punishing, scapegoating, snickering family members!* We are two years old, starting to express ourselves in the world, and getting shot down! We're heckled, ridiculed, ignored, sometimes even physically attacked.

Again, this is almost never the reality. Nevertheless, stage fright can be so severe that people turn to drastic solutions—most of which don't work.

Fear Band-Aids

Almost everybody gets stage fright—even seasoned professional speakers. Many of them learn to bulldoze through the fear with bravado, or to cover it up with "professional techniques," fancy footwork, and exacting preparation—but this usually keeps them from really connecting with the audience. If the speaker is putting up a front, the audience has to put up a front as well.

These Fear Band-Aids are not the answer to stage fright. At heart, these speakers are usually still scared. When something goes wrong or something unexpected happens, their composure slips. Even when nothing goes wrong, listeners sense that something is missing. It's as if the speaker is not really live, but on tape. That act is wearing thin in today's marketplace, and will wear out completely in the marketplace of the future, as people become less and less likely to trust a polished facade.

Being willing to let others see where we are, even when we're scared, *defines* an authentic relationship. But speakers who depend on "holding it all together" are terrified of this prospect and are apt to reach for a Fear Band-Aid instead.

What to do: embrace the shakes

There is nothing shameful about stage fright. Everyone in the audience has experienced it, and they are thankful that we're standing up in front instead of them. If we can be with the fear and move through it, we act as surrogates for them. We are conquering their past and future stage fright for them, right before their eyes, and they appreciate us for it.

If we avoid resisting or hiding the fear, it can actually bond us to the audience. Transformational Speaking teaches us to notice, accept, and respect our fear. That stretches us, and the audience knows it. They're rooting for us.

To move beyond stage fright organically, naturally, honestly, and in a way that builds connection with the audience, we simply stand before them and feel the fear. In Speaking Circles, we might talk about it. In a public speaking situation, we probably wouldn't. But in any case, we need to keep breathing in their support. That support grows with every second, letting us reach more deeply into our own wisdom, and we start to feel more at ease. As the electricity builds between us and the audience, we feel more relaxed and focused on why we are there. Of course, all of this is much easier if we have practiced it well in Speaking Circles. One healer says,

> I had tremendous fear of speaking in front of groups of even three or four people—tight throat, heart palpitations, the works. I wanted to expand my teaching of headache relief to both lecture and workshop formats, but the fear was keeping me back. During my first Speaking Circle, I got up and nervously blubbered my way through 3 minutes as I had always done. It felt lousy. Next time, I tried just getting up there and facing my fear. Just being in it. I sat down on the stage because I could hardly stand, and said something about just being in my fear. Then I just sat there.

> I looked around the room from face to face and received support from people whom I didn't even know, and they were also receiving me. Not just the "public" me, but the

vulnerable me. My vision of the room changed to rosy and, I'd have to say, almost psychedelic-energy filled. People gave feedback on how beautiful a person I am. I was later able to confirm it on my videotape. I felt very seen and accepted. It was a very healing moment for me and marked a turning point in my speaking ability and general comfort level in groups.

For me, it seems to have to do with accepting myself right where I am. No matter what happens, I'll still love myself.

Stage fright tips

Here are a few tips that I've discovered, or that people have shared with me, for dealing with stage fright.

1. Live in the present.

Fear almost always has to do with future events, and most stage fright happens before we get to the stage. It's actually the fear that we're going to be on-stage, rather than the fact of actually being on-stage. Sometimes just realizing this is enough to dissipate stage fright.

Many speakers have certain rituals or routines to center themselves before they go "on." These might include positive acknowledgment for themselves, some form of meditation, or reminders that they can trust their connection with the audience.

2. Breathe.

Many people get stage fright because they don't breathe. Or they breathe in, but don't exhale fully— so they start to hyperventilate. Take some deep breaths, and remember to breathe out all the way. Think of breathing in the audience, making their beauty part of you, and then breathing out grace in their direction.

3. *Visualize.*

People have shared with me that they visualize and recreate images and feelings of positive Speaking Circle experiences before speaking to larger groups—or think of a special person or a higher power to put the event in perspective.

4. *Remember that stage fright is universal.*

Anxiety on-stage or "in the spotlight" is normal and healthy. It's just energy, and you can use it to your advantage.

5. *Just do it.*

Sometimes we just have to jump into the water, rather than stand shivering on the diving board. We have to find a quiet place within ourselves, and open up to the group. That's where we'll find our peace, our connection, and our center.

Receiving makes us strong

Putting our attention on others almost always relieves stress, and this is particularly true in public speaking. When we focus on receiving the people in front of us, we naturally become less self-conscious. The more we put our attention on them, the more comfortable and confident we feel.

According to one trainer,

> I was a wreck because I was always thinking about "What am I going to say? How am I going to come off? How am I going to do?" The first thing I do now is remind myself that there are real people out there, people I want to honor and attend to. I take a few minutes to really look at them and take in their support. Even if I feel shut down, I open up so I can receive them. That changes everything. In that moment, we're connected on a deeper level than I'm often connected with my co-workers or friends. There's so much satisfaction in connecting with people from that heart place that it doesn't matter if I'm nervous.

Fear never goes away completely for most of us, but we have something that is stronger than the fear. We trust that if we connect with our audience, if we start that electrical current, we will know what to say and be able to say it effectively. When we put our attention on those people, our relationship with them takes over and the stage fright starts to slip away. Over time, that feeling of connection becomes more attractive than the fear of being on-stage.

"Stage fright? I was the poster boy," says a successful professional speaker and entertainer. "I always felt nervous, with dry mouth, having to pee, shaking, forgetful. But there's a part of me now that's just eager to get out there and connect. The excitement and anticipation is greater than the fear."

It's a little like the anxiety an athlete feels before the big game— a little nervous from all the raw energy, but full of anticipation to pour that energy into the moment of truth.

"I used to rely on the content of the talk as my security blanket and focus on delivering the information," said an advertising executive. "But I'm a lot more comfortable now that I concentrate on the relationship with the audience."

Defusing the inner critic

The inner critic is that negative voice within us that constantly criticizes us or puts us down. When we're in front of the room, the inner critic sits on our shoulder, judging everything we say and do. Each of us has a tailor-made version of this little heckler who points directly at our most secret imperfections, and aims his taunts at precisely the weaknesses we most want to conceal from others.

We don't want to kill off the inner critic. It is just one of many voices within us, and can actually be helpful at times. The inner critic is the one who keeps us from screaming at inappropriate moments, throwing food on the wall, or performing other embarrassing acts. We need to give the inner critic its voice, but not let it make decisions for us or make us miserable.

The best way to work with the inner critic is to let it have its say—but not to let it have the *final* say, and not to take every word it utters as the truth. Fighting the inner critic only makes it stronger and feeds it power. We need to accept the inner critic, but not take it too seriously or let it run the show.

When we're in front of the room, we can let the inner critic jabber away without paying too much attention to it. It becomes like the background noise of a television that nobody's really watching. If it keeps turning up the volume and distracts us from our message or our connection with the audience, we can defuse it by actually giving it voice. We can say something like, "My inner critic is hammering at me about this shirt being the wrong color and about not preparing enough," or "A part of me feels that you're all better educated than I am..." Or the inner critic might have judgments about our not having lost that 20 pounds, or about having a crooked smile, or not being "good with people," or likable, or smart enough, or any of a thousand negative judgments.

Remember: it's not the crime; it's the cover-up. It's not the inner critic that's so terrible; it's that we're denying it, judging it, embarrassed by it, or trying to cover it up. The problem is not the inner critic, it's our inner criticism of the inner critic.

Even when there's something to what the inner critic is saying, we have to remember that *it has a very narrow perspective*. Maybe we *would* look better without those 20 pounds, but that doesn't mean people aren't going to be moved and inspired by what we say. Maybe we could have prepared more, but perhaps people can only take in as much as we brought with us today. Maybe we aren't as charming as our baby sister, but perhaps charm isn't the best quality to bring to this particular material.

We can defuse the inner critic not only by accepting it, but by reinforcing the larger picture. Our weaknesses are not all that we are. If we let our "inner cheerleader" out, perhaps that cheerleader would have even more to say than the critic. We need to hold those criticisms in the context of all our strengths. The inner critic can stick around, but it has to be part of the orchestra and not take over.

The inner critic also tries to get our attention *after* we speak— and we can use the same antidotes. A writer and consultant told me, "I gave a talk at one of those high-tech luncheons about advertising. It was pretty good, but right in the middle, I lost my train of thought. The great feeling that I love in talks, the connection, broke momentarily. Probably nobody noticed, but on the way home, that was the only thing I could think of. My focus was not on the 59 minutes when I was doing a good job. It was on the ten seconds when I felt I lost control."

As we begin to notice how our critic works, we can move its voice into the "background noise" and start feeding the positive aspects of ourselves with attention. When we humor and embrace it without giving it power, and keep what it says in perspective, then we will always be senior to it.

"I used to listen to the screeching, judgmental voices of my internal nitpickers, filling my head with negativity as I tried to speak," says singer and songwriter Jana Stanfield. "It is a joy to hear, instead, a gentle affirming voice filling my heart with courage...and I can now quiet an audience of rowdy teenagers without saying a word."

Michelle Balk is a psychotherapist who attended a weekly San Francisco Speaking Circle for two years before relocating to Paris in August 1996, where she hopes to initiate the first French Circle. Here is an excerpt from her final talk, in which she gives insight into the successful defusing of an inner critic.

> I will be affected by this work for the rest of my life. It will always influence and inform who I become.
>
> When I first came here, I remember being so frightened, so frightened of getting up and being judged. That was probably one of the more terrifying experiences of growing up the way I grew up, because I felt a lot of judgment; there *was* a lot of judgment.
>
> I would come to this Circle, do my thing, and like a lot of you folks I would just speak wherever I was, whether it was crying or laughing or whatever—and I would walk away full of my own judgments. They weren't *your* judgments; they were *mine*—about me. Sometimes I thought they came from other people but they actually came very much from me.
>
> That particular burden is mostly gone now, because I know my own truth. I know who I am. I know what I'm

doing. I know my intent. I know it so solidly now, and I credit this Speaking Circle process with a lot of that.

I can stand in my own truth facing whatever judgments somebody might have, and I don't cringe and want to run any more. I really feel solid in my own self, and confident in what I know to be true about myself, and I feel that that's come in large measure from doing this work.

The inner critic visits a Speaking Circle

The best way I know to defuse the inner critic is through Speaking Circles. Positive feedback makes the inner critic very quiet. One Speaking Circle veteran says, "In Speaking Circles, my inner critic gets very lonely." Nobody else in the room is buying what it says, because there is nothing voiced but support and positive acknowledgment.

One of the inner critic's favorite tricks is to compare us with other people. Since we don't voice that in Circles, the critic is disarmed in a very substantial way.

The inner critic gets even lonelier when we watch our tapes, and see the beauty that emerges when we come out into the group's support. The critic may be pretty noisy the *first* time we watch our tapes. "See?! You're fat! You're tongue-tied! You don't know what to do with your hands!"

But by the second and third time we watch a tape, the other voices have their turn. We can't deny that there is connection, warmth, and bottom-line lovability. No matter how many times the critic jumps up and down screaming, "You're bad, you're bad, you're bad," we can see with our own eyes that it's just not true. That helps us take everything the inner critic says in the future with a grain of salt.

Retired real estate appraiser Grant Flint tells how Speaking Circles helped him manage chronic stage fright.

> After 10 weeks in a phobia class and over 200 speeches in four Toastmasters clubs, I still suffered from fundamental stage fright. The audience was the "enemy," a faceless mob ready to ridicule and humiliate me. I felt completely alone

in front of people. The Speaking Circle was a chance to be myself with others for the first time in my life. I hadn't done that with my wives, my children, or closest friends. It was a chance to experiment, with positive feedback, to explore the various aspects and contradictions in myself, to be completely open and vulnerable in a safe setting.

After that unconditional love and acceptance, people tell me I'm more calm, less compulsive, more effective, and seem more happy. I've found a direction and simple meaning in my life—becoming more and more myself, not only in front of other people, but with myself. I'm not only more confident, but I can be more loving.

As a speaker, all audiences seem friendly to me now. I connect easily one-on-one with members of any audience. I feel more honest, humble, vulnerable, human, and intimate with the people to whom I speak. My stage fright is 10%; my delight in being on stage being myself, loving people, and being loved is 90%. And my secret extrovert has come out of the closet. Being myself is everything.

Easy acts to follow

It is common for a Speaking Circle newcomer, when called upon to take the stage after a particularly wonderful talk, to start by muttering glumly, "That's a tough act to follow."

This line inspires a groan from the regulars, who have come to understand its self-defeating absurdity. And they know it's the one line that I, as facilitator, have trouble letting pass without an interruption and a lecture that breaks my own rules.

"That's a tough act to follow" comes from the competitive inner critic at its most devious and cunning. In fact, the audience is making no such comparison. If they are enchanted by one speaker being exactly who *he* is, they are that much more ready for the next speaker to be exactly who *she* is.

I learned this lesson in the innocent days of San Francisco stand-up comedy in the late 1970s, when I was a perspiring comedian hiding behind my jokes. "That's a tough act to follow" was our predominant mind-set. Most of dreaded following a great set, as few and far between as they were in those days.

Then a new comic named Robin Williams showed up and broke the mold. I was there for his first "open mike" opportunity, and the audience response gave no indication of how successful he would become. But he rooted for the rest of us, reveled in our victories, and within weeks found his stride. He seemed to love surfing the energy waves generated by the prior acts and taking it through the roof. He made us all better with his positive outlook. I began to notice how hopeful and eager an audience looked when I followed someone who had uplifted them. *But I had to look.* If I didn't look, the inner critic turned a great advantage into a deficit by making irrational comparisons.

In Speaking Circles, we come to root for each other without reservation, and we learn to love "surfing the stage" after it has been graced by a *tour de force.*

Look before you speak: miracle cure for stage fright

The quickest turnaround from agony to ecstasy I've ever seen was at a workshop I conducted for psychotherapists. After sharing my ideas about Transformational Speaking with them, followed by small circle exercises, I had a few participants address the entire group. Then I asked for a volunteer who had such severe stage fright they *dreaded* the thought of coming up, but knew they needed to move past this block to speak effectively about their practice.

A red-faced young woman rose and came to the front of the room on trembling legs, amazed and horrified that she had answered the call. I handed her the microphone and sat in the front row to coach. I said, "Look at us and just take in our support."

With eyes glued to the floor, she muttered, "I'm so scared."

I said, "No, please just look at us."

She lifted her eyes, they widened, and instantly a huge smile spread over her face as she said, "I'm not scared." From that point, her words flowed and her spirit soared.

In 5 seconds, she had experienced the subtle shift in focus that moved her through a lifetime of stage fright into a future of grace under pressure—the shift from anxiety about *giving*, to relaxing into *receiving*.

Death, taxes, and stage fright: making friends with fear

Stage fright is a fact of life. It will always be with us, but it doesn't have to stop us from having a good time or from speaking effectively. We may always feel an undercurrent of timidity when we think of speaking in public, but we can take inspiration from Eleanor Roosevelt, who used to tell people, "It's alright to be shy, just don't let it get in the way of doing things."

Fear isn't something we get rid of, in speaking or in life. But we can make friends with fear. We can practice not letting it stop us or make us miserable. To help us, we have the strongest force in the universe: love. What lets us live with fear is the knowledge that we can rise above it through our connections with people.

"I used to try getting over my stage fright," says a graphologist (handwriting expert), "but now I see that fear as a place to *explore*. A place where I can learn more about myself. I've made a lot of money in the past year and a half, testifying in court as expert witness. Before Circles, I would have let fear keep me from doing that. I'm also enjoying myself more at parties and family gatherings. I'm letting the extrovert out of the closet."

Making friends with stage fright is one of the most exciting things about Speaking Circles. When we've done that, we can handle even the difficult audiences described in the next chapter. ◎

Chapter 10

Creating Support in Any Audience

You've done it all—learned to drop into the place where you are most authentic, practiced opening up, receiving, and connecting with your audience. You're healing your Inner Speaker and making friends with stage fright.

Then, *disaster strikes*. You find yourself in front of a nightmare group, in circumstances that even Winston Churchill or Mother Teresa would find challenging. It might be:

- The hemorrhaging crowd who have just learned their company is downsizing and they may well lose their jobs
- The after-dinner crowd, sleepy from too much food and drink, tired after a day of listening to speakers—and if they have to talk to anybody, they're only interested in promoting themselves
- The lunchtime crowd who have just been served their entrees as you are introduced, who are wielding the noisiest knives and forks in creation and chatting with one another about the texture of the pasta or the baked chicken—and could care less about the lonely figure in the front of the room
- The crowd you never imagined, for whom you should never have been hired as a speaker—you are speaking on vegetarianism to spouses at a Texas cattlemen's convention, or to New York bill collectors on gentle support in the workplace.

Disaster can also come in individually wrapped packages. One person—a drunk, a heckler, an unruly uninvited guest, a person who has to take over any room he is in—can present a challenge to even the most serene and centered speaker.

This chapter is about how to create support in any room. It is about tough audiences, speaking nightmares, worst-case scenarios—and how to turn them all into wins.

Where support begins

The truth is that most audiences are neutral, at worst. They are usually either indifferent or mildly interested, and a few start out enthusiastic. But when we're standing alone at the podium or the conference table, everybody can start looking like Atilla the Hun. Sometimes our fears have some foundation—but we need to enter every room knowing that, regardless of what we find, we can create support for ourselves and our message.

Support begins with us. It's up to us to bring the support we've gotten in Speaking Circles into any room where we speak. The more we practice receiving, and the more we've come to expect support, the easier that becomes.

Richard and Antra Borofsky are Transformational Speakers and psychologists in Boston who specialize in relationships. What they say about one-to-one relationships applies to the speaker-audience relationship as well: "We usually think that to receive something, there has to be somebody who has something to give. But if the receiver is a skillful receiver, he or she can actually *create* what they want to receive. They can create the giving in the other person. We teach that good receivers make good givers."

The truth is that, in any room, there are people who do want to support us. They may not be the first people we see, or the people on whom we first focus, but they are there. Somebody is biting into her chicken, thinking, "Oh, that must be tough on the person up there, to be speaking just as we start eating. I'll send a smile or give that person my attention." Another person remembers when he was in a similar difficult position in front of the room or in a meeting, and sends some goodwill.

We need to recognize these people, to seek out the pockets of support that exist in any room, and focus on them. We need to open up the electrical current between them and us, so that it becomes the focal point and everyone else is irresistibly drawn into it.

Focus, Revisit, Spread

One friendly face

Even in the most difficult rooms, there are usually one or two friendly faces. It's up to us to find those people, and speak directly to them. That one supportive connection becomes infectious. Before long, we've brought the whole audience along with us and created a network of good feelings. That connection is bound to be more interesting and more pleasant than anything else that's going on. When we receive the support that's available, other people get the idea—even when they don't look like they will.

A university professor who had spent decades in front of classrooms found a whole new level of connection by singling out the one supportive person in an audience: "The idea of taking a moment to receive the support that is naturally there, then connect with one person who is most clearly supportive and start talking to that person, was a breakthrough for me. As an introvert, I'm at my best talking to one person at a time."

"I look for the one person with whom I feel safe," says a contractor and community leader. "Speak to that person, build the energy, and spread it from there. I can usually draw out at least one to three people. I'll see a glimmer in the eye or a nod of the head, and I'll stay with that person, let it grow to the person next to them and get some interaction going."

The corollary to the "One Friendly Face" guideline is *not* to focus on the one *unfriendly* face. A therapist told me:

> At a talk about a year ago for the child abuse council, there was one person in the audience who never cracked a smile and didn't seem to like me. These were all social workers, and case workers, teachers, and therapists. I thought this woman hated my guts. I realized I had a choice: I could focus on her, or on the other 40 people in the room. I

could drop inside, notice what was throwing me off track, and do what works—go for the support. I can just be who I am, deliver what I have, and let it fall where it may.

I trust that process more each time I speak.

The power of trust

When we walk to the front of the room, we can't ask ourselves, "Will these people support me, or not?" We need to know we are the source of that support, and that we can find that one friendly face. If we don't see it right away, we just hang in there until we do.

We don't wait to see if it's a "tough audience" or an "easy audience." We trust that we can allow *every* audience to become a supportive one.

Speaking Circles are the best place to develop this trust. Once we've experience that level of support, over and over again, we come to expect it. And the greater our expectation of support, the easier it is to create support in a room that is *not* operating with the instruction to support us. Through our expectation and trust, we actually train people to be there for us.

"When I open up, I'm inviting people to support me," says an advertising executive. "When the support comes, it invites me to open up even more. It just keeps getting better and better."

"Trouble" in the audience:
the graduate school of public speaking

What if we have a heckler or drunk in the audience? Or someone who is better behaved than a heckler, but challenges us at every turn. Or people who sit sullenly, with their arms and legs crossed? Or people who walk out?

Every audience is like a living organism, made of many different aspects of humanity—which are also various aspects of ourselves. If one part of the organism is giving us trouble, our instinct may be to defend against it, to fight back, or to actively ignore it. We may be tempted to try controlling the situation by having Security throw the bum out, or by arguing him or her down until we are the clear victor.

This is rarely the best approach. When we pit ourselves against the person who is acting out, that person comes to represent the whole audience. By fighting him, we set up a dynamic in which we're using our power on the podium to pick on the little guy—and by extension, the whole audience. Their instinct will be to defend him.

We need to remember that the "problem person" is only one part of the organism. He may be like a cancer, but the larger organism has ways to fight cancer. Speakers who try to cut out or beat down the troublesome person put their whole attention on the problem and give it power. They forget about the immune system.

As Transformational Speakers, we work with the immune system to heal the organism. We embrace the individual wherever he is—crazy, hostile, wanting to leave—and treat him with dignity and respect. No matter how vicious or problematic the person becomes, we keep accepting and supporting him.

We model good behavior. We use the problem as part of our presentation. We treat the situation as an example of what we are saying, and model the behavior we are suggesting to the audience. We embrace the opportunity to demonstrate our message, and so we don't get frightened of the person. We don't resist him or defend against him. We are open to him, hear him, and stay connected to him.

The rest of the room sees this, and gets behind us. When their energy aligns with ours, either the problem person will be swept back into the goodwill of the group, or he will leave. The audience is the immune system, and works with us one way or another to solve the problem. We're on the same side, working together for the good of the organism and all its parts.

Allowing for magic

To deal in an accepting, supportive way with difficulties, we have to let go of our expectations about how the talk should go. We have to play the hand we're dealt, and make the best of it. The talk may turn out differently from what it would have been without that person in the audience, but we trust that it went the way it was supposed to go—and almost always it turns out to be better than it would have been without the trouble.

All we can do is stand in our own light, work with the energy, and let it go. Some people come around, others at least quiet down, and some really do have to be taken away by Security in the end. But if we've stood in the light regardless of what was out there, we have at least taken the high road. One thing is certain: Being reactive in the face of a problem in the audience will only make the situation worse.

Again, it's like aikido. In this martial art, you don't fight or run from negative energy; you work with it and redirect it. Aikido experts believe that aggressive energy comes from a wounded place in the other person, and that it dissipates if you really connect with that person's true center.

A career counselor put it this way: "The way I speak to an audience that doesn't seem to be in agreement with me is to be in agreement with myself, in touch with myself, and the fact that I'm okay."

Another way to connect with any audience is humor—but especially in difficult situations, we have to make sure it's humor of the heart, not humor of the head or the spleen. The next chapter discusses the difference. ◎

Chapter 11

The Laughing Spirit: Healthy Humor

We all have the Laughing Spirit. It is that place deep within us of love, connection, and amusement at our predicament as human beings.

The Laughing Spirit is released whenever we break the "illusion of separation" among us, and remind ourselves in a light way that we all share the same human foibles, and that we're all connected. My favorite Laughing Spirit joke is a riddle:

How do you make God laugh? Tell him your plans.

We're all a little lost, if the truth be known, and the Laughing Spirit is able to be light about that fact and even make it an adventure. It acknowledges the chaos that lives within each of us. Scientists say that the order of the universe is chaos. I think it's possible that each of us is a universe of chaos. The Laughing Spirit addresses that.

People feel comfortable and relaxed around us when we can laugh gently at our own pretensions and be compassionate about the pretensions of others.

Three kinds of humor

Humor comes in three flavors. Each evokes a different kind of laughter: Laughter of the Head, Laughter of the Spleen, and Laughter of the Heart.

1. *Laughter of the Head*

Laughter of the Head is evoked by cleverness and wit. It often involves wordplay, irony, light jokes, or esoteric references and allusions. It's not harmful in small doses, but it tends to become competitive. One person plays off the last person's comment, and the conversation becomes a duel of intellects. It's a mode of humor that encourages one-upsmanship.

Laughter of the Head also tends to exclude those who are a little slow on the uptake, not verbally oriented, or from other cultures where the joke doesn't necessarily translate. This kind of humor can jeopardize the sense of community in an audience, because the atmosphere isn't always safe when glibness prevails. When anything that's said may be turned into a pun or witticism, people put up their guard.

Heady humor can keep people at a distance. We all know someone who feels compelled to be "on" all the time—but never shares very deeply and often doesn't say what he or she really means. No one else in that environment feels safe to share honest emotions or vulnerabilities, either.

Children are often "humor abused" with Laughter of the Head. A 6-year-old says at the dinner table, "I want to be a fireman when I grow up." His father fires back, "Well then you can start by hosing down the dishes in the sink." It's funny and draws a laugh, but the little boy doesn't get the joke. He just feels defeated, confused, and mildly put down—and he may disappear into himself.

From the platform, clever lines may win the battle for laughs but lose the war for our audience's hearts—and hearts are what move minds and bodies to action.

The old conventional wisdom for speakers was to open with a joke, and it usually involved Laughter of the Head. A speaker on health might say, "Did you hear about recent studies showing an increase in heart disease in China? I'm not surprised, with all those Taipei (Type A) personalities!" That would probably get a laugh, but perhaps at the cost of some audience trust.

People may smile and chuckle on cue at head humor, but inwardly they may feel we are trying to impress them, and they become resentful. Why turn people off or make them feel distrustful when we can tell a humorous personal story that includes everyone?

In the end, Laughter of the Head is usually stressful—even for those who are good at delivering it.

2. Laughter of the Spleen

Laughter of the Spleen is evoked by humor at the expense of a person or group. It may involve sexist, ageist, or racist put-downs, sexual innuendo, sarcasm, hostility, and barbs that pit people against one another. Many television sitcoms and stand-up comics rely on Laughter of the Spleen.

Laughter of the Spleen makes most people uncomfortable, even when they don't show it, because nobody knows when the meanness will turn against *them*. Anybody could be the butt of the next joke. It tends to create an unhealthy atmosphere, especially at work. Sexual innuendo has taken the longest fall from grace, because it not only makes the workplace unproductive but can be cited in sexual harassment lawsuits.

David Garfinkel, copywriter and co-author of *Guerilla Direct Mail Marketing*, says that in the workplace of the future, "The old slap-on-the-back salesman with the raunchy jokes that put down women will no longer make it—at all, anywhere. But the person who can come in and tell a story, express a sentiment, convey a feeling with words or with an attitude that reinforces the sense of community, is going to win. He or she will get the promotions, build longer-term relationships, earn a higher income, and get more satisfaction from the job."

3. *Laughter of the Heart*

Laughter of the Heart results from humor of The Laughing Spirit. It recognizes in a light-hearted, good-natured way that we are all human, and that we all have great strengths and wild foibles. It bows to the human condition, and includes everybody. Laughter flows when we all share the embarrassment of the human experience.

Healthy humor observes the chatter of our minds, and reveals the hilarious secret that none of us has it all together, even though we all *pretend* to have it together. Bill Cosby, Lily Tomlin, Garrison Keillor, and Tom Hanks in a role such as "Forrest Gump" are examples of Laughter of the Heart people. So are my early role models, Mike Nichols and Elaine May, who were funny because they told the truth about how men and women really interact with one another. All find their humor in the truth of human nature.

Laughter of the Heart is relaxing and good for morale in the office. It breaks tension, and makes everyone feel more whole and productive. It reinforces the feeling that we're all in this together, and hinges on high self-esteem.

Jokes and cleverness can easily and quickly turn into bad business. Being human is funny enough, and "non-toxic" heart humor opens up the audience to our message, information, or inspiration.

Laughter makes us whole

Why do we laugh? Researchers tell us that laughter is our natural response to releasing tension or conflict—even when we are not consciously aware of what that tension or conflict may be.

I believe that the fundamental human tension is between two aspects of our nature: the spiritual part of us that knows we're all one, and the part of us that forgets this. Hundreds of times a day, we forget our higher selves and succumb to alienation, victimhood, misunderstanding, aloneness, resentment, and anxiety.

Releasing the tension between these two parts of ourselves basically means slipping back into our spiritual selves, where we realize our wholeness and our unity with other people. As soon as that second aspect is lifted, even for a moment, the tension is relieved. There is an explosion of natural humor—whether it's smile, a guffaw, or just a good feeling. Sometimes it's just an "Aha!" Or an "Oh yeah, we're alike!"

No matter how many times, or how fully, we return to our higher selves, the tension always builds right back up again. This means we have unlimited opportunities to break it again and laugh. The Laughing Spirit is always just beneath the surface, reminding us that we're connected with ourselves and with others. The actual laughter happens whenever that Spirit breaks through.

"I recently addressed a group of about fifty young people in transition from the military to civilian life on the advantages of owning one's own business," says one professional speaker. "They were a little frightened about the prospect, and the group didn't really open up to me until we all laughed together at one example of how I'd failed."

Circle Speaker and humorist David Roche brings people together by sharing his own particular twist on universal conditions and fears.

> They laugh not when I make jokes, but when I just talk about what's going on with me. Things like what it's like to be in the male menopause with cold flashes, or God's cruel joke that as we all get older, women get more interested in sex and men get less interested—and there's only one 3-week period when we're on the same page. People feel safe because I'm talking about my own fears, but they may have either those same fears or *parallel* fears. And normally people don't talk about this stuff.

Donna Strickland is a nurse and humorist who conducts "Laughing Spirit Speaking Circles" at nursing homes in Denver. She has a profound perspective on healthy humor.

> I see humor as having a fluid spirit. Laughter is a discharge of tension, and it's based on relationship with the audience. People who are perfectly polished in their speaking, who have to be completely in control, have trouble with that relationship—because you can't plan ahead exactly what you're going to do. There's no roadmap for spon-

taneous humor that just bubbles up. That kind of humor requires that you let go of control, that you flow and flex with what is funny to you and to your audience in the moment.

Finding the Laughing Spirit

I coined the phrase "Laughing Spirit" when I was in Italy in 1980. I had just separated from my first wife after a year of marriage, and it was the worst time of my life.

We had been writing comedy together for television, and she had suddenly stopped laughing at my jokes. I lost my identity as a clever guy, a funny guy, and I was really miserable. I had to get out of the house, out of the relationship, and out of the country, so I decided to go to Europe.

For the first couple weeks there, I had a very bad attitude and a terrible time. I had lost my sense of humor, and nothing about Europe worked for me. But then one morning at 7:00 a.m., I was jolted awake when our train stopped at a little town just over the Italian border. I opened my eyes for another day of satisfying sulking, but what I saw outside the train window changed my perspective and brought me into The Laughing Spirit.

Two Italian trainmen in full uniform were having an animated conversation on the platform, waving their arms and gesturing wildly. I couldn't hear what they were saying, but it was obvious that they were living their lives passionately and humorously, in the spirit of full humanity, even at 7:00 in the morning. As the train pulled away, I started letting their joy and vitality come into me, and suddenly I knew that something was going to change that day.

I was sharing a compartment with an Italian family of four. I didn't speak any Italian, and they didn't speak any English. I took out my traveler's phrasebook, which until then I had used only to order food, and decided to have some fun. I turned to the list of common things you could say in Italian—things like hello, goodbye, excuse me—and I said, *"Mi scusi!"*

They all looked at me with great anticipation and said, *"Si, senore?"*

The next phrase was "Good morning," so I said in my best Brooklyn accent, *"Bon giorno!"*

They all said with great ebullience, *"Bon giorno, senore!!"*

The next entry that applied was, "I don't speak Italian." *"Non parlo Italiano."* They laughed uproariously. Apparently, this was obvious. The next phrase was, "I'm lost." I certainly was lost in my life, so I said, *"Non se dove mi trovo."*

They sighed, clutched their hands together, and said, *"OOhh, senore!"* They felt my pain! I was connecting!

The next sentence was, "Which way shall I go?" *"In quale direzione devo andare?"* And with that, all four of them pointed dramatically in the direction the train was going. Suddenly, I was laughing!

I laughed the rest of the trip, in trains all over Europe, in four languages. I was still lost in my life, but I was connecting with people in the universal language of laughter that brings us together. I had finally met The Laughing Spirit, the common humanity that joins us all together in being lost.

When we connect with someone in this Laughing Spirit, we immediately get the heart connection—no matter what language we're speaking. It's not always about laughing; it's just a light-hearted connection that acknowledges that we're all lost, but we're together.

Embracing the darkness

Humor isn't always about the light side of life. At the bottom of everything are both laughter and tears, and sometimes we can get to the laughter by allowing ourselves the tears.

In Speaking Circles, people often talk about the shadow side of their lives, and end up stepping into the light. When they do that, we all experience the catharsis and the transformation. We walk into the light with them.

Our funniest stories may draw tears the first time we tell them, but eventually the laughter comes through.

Forced laughter

The best humor is rarely planned. The old paradigm for humor is selling jokes; the new paradigm is telling stories.

Jokes can make an effective point when they are told skillfully and are particularly appropriate to the subject, but attempts to *make* a group laugh can backfire. Audiences tend to feel manipulated, resistant, distrustful, and even resentful when we *ask* them to laugh, *pressure* them to laugh, or feel embarrassed or disappointed if they don't laugh.

Whenever we expect, demand, or leave space for a laugh in our script—and whenever we say something that we wouldn't say except to get a laugh—we've betrayed our relationship with them in some subtle way. We've broken the connection that is at the heart of Transformational Speaking.

The contrived joke may get a laugh that's a "ha ha" from the head, but people often withhold the "ho ho's" from their hearts and the "hardy har har's" from their bellies.

When we tell a clever, snappy joke that doesn't really go anywhere, with the intention just to "loosen up the audience," we are actually creating distrust. People aren't sure where we're going; all they know is that we started off by trying to manipulate them into something.

Reaching "the giddy innards"

To get the really good laugh, we want to be playful. We reach people's giddy innards by relaxing them with accounts of our own humanity, by letting them know that we are one of them, and by reliving our vulnerable moments, close calls, and poignant incidents with career and family. They open up when we tell stories from our daily lives, true stories of heart, soul, and common foibles.

At a humor program I conducted for psychotherapists, a participant said, "I just can't seem to get to my humor, and I want to change that." When I had her address the group, she was deadly serious about being deadly serious. So I asked her just to talk to us about the stress of not being funny, and wanting to be funny. The pressure was off, and she started a natural riff that cracked everybody up.

We don't have to work for laughter; it is always abundantly available. In fact, we're repressing a natural laughter all the time—and that pressure is released when we simply tell people in our own way, at a leisurely pace, about real life experiences, attitudes, limitations, personal paradoxes or challenges.

Our own amusement at our predicament activates their natural laughter. When we tell the truth from the platform, without blame or shame, we automatically trigger corresponding stories in the audience's lives. They remember that they are not alone and feel no resistance to laughing in communion with us. We've broken the tension of isolation—between us and them, and between the light and dark parts of all of us.

Of course, we need to get the hang of reliving our stories, rather than simply memorizing them, and of picking the right stories for the right occasion and connecting them to our topic or message. But this natural humor eventually works even for presenters who don't think they are funny and who have never had the knack of telling a joke well.

The rule of thumb is this: Never reach for a laugh or try to orchestrate a response. No laugh is worth risking credibility by appearing to manipulate the audience. Think of "letting people laugh" rather than "making people laugh." Humor always shows up when we respect and like our audience, and when we talk about things that genuinely amuse us. Our own amusement becomes infectious.

Dare to be boring

When I coached comedy, I always told people that who we are is funny enough, and they should just tell the truth and dare to be boring. Most comedians are addicted to laughter, so this was nearly impossible for them—but giving ourselves permission not to be funny opens up endless possibilities for humor.

Conventional speaking wisdom tells us that we should use humor to lighten people up, provide a change of pace, and relax the audience. But we can do all those things simply by being real and connecting. We can just stop and smile because somebody out there is sending us a friendly thought. That's a humor break, even if there is no laughter. It produces the same result of relieving tension. Transformational Speakers don't need humor, and so they tend to draw laughs.

One Speaker reports, "I did a presentation for a civic group, and several months later got a call to come emcee their awards presentation because I was a humorist. I hadn't meant my civic group talk to be particularly funny. I was just being natural and telling my own stories."

All humor should be that natural. The Laughing Spirit is our natural state. The way to tap it is simply to be ourselves. ◎

Chapter 12

Transformational Speaking in Business

Connecting, listening, and authenticity are the new paradigms in American business.

Entrepreneurs, business leaders, and newcomers with a dream are all called on to hold forth at a moment's notice in meeting rooms, media rooms, restaurants, elevators, and around the water cooler. Our presentation skills are on display all day, every day. From planned speeches to spontaneous pep talks, better business requires instant rapport. We have to connect immediately with people's hearts and minds, in our own unique styles, so that our words hit home and get results.

"Every person who's come to the Speaking Circle has told me that it generated more income for them," Circle leader Gayla Alders says.

One corporate trainer wrote:

> Last week I was one of a panel of three speakers talking about telemarketing techniques. The other two speakers went first, and I watched listeners' eyes glaze over because these guys were just rattling out information. The whole audience was frowning because they weren't getting their questions answered or their needs met.
>
> When it was my turn, I looked right into their eyes and announced that I would begin by addressing their questions first, then talk about what has worked for me. They lit up! I let them tell me what they wanted to know, and they scrib-

bled furiously when I answered. Afterward, people thanked
me for being so direct and to the point, and for saving them
from a whole seminar of boredom.

Transformational Speaking skills enhance almost every aspect
of business: management, meetings, training, marketing, team
building, customer service, diversity, and media relations.

The new paradigm in business

People in Speaking Circles sometimes ask, "Yeah, all this soulful
connection is great in a safe space, but what about when I go back
to the office? How do you bring that into a public presentation in
the business arena?"

I believe that, at its highest levels, business is conducted on the
basis of personal relationships and connections. If I were putting
millions into a project, I would want to look into my associates'
eyes and see someone authentic at home in there.

"Public speaking skill has risen to the top of nearly every company's wish list of executive attributes," Hal Lancaster says in his
January 9, 1996, *Wall Street Journal* column on "Managing Your
Career." "Why? 'As organizations are downsizing, we need more
well-rounded people,' says Hollis Church, a vice president of Com-
munispond, which provides presentation training for executives.
'They may not only be the technical expert, but the spokesperson
for a product.'"

The *Journal* said again, in a December 14, 1992, article on trends
in book publishing: "The CEOs of the future will be those who
manage through shared values rather than directives of fear. When
it comes to business books, the 80s are definitely over. Greed is
out, ethics is in."

Authenticity is being touted as one of the most effective leadership tools around. In an age of cynicism and distrust, it is one of
the few things that inspire people to action. To get authentic commitment from people, we need to inspire them with genuine passion. What we say doesn't count for much if people don't believe
us, or if they don't think that we believe *ourselves*. Today, enlight-

ened business leaders build trust and get results by revealing their authentic selves and setting an inspired example.

The new paradigm in business is to build trust and produce results by being ourselves, honestly listening to the people we serve, and inspiring by our honest passion and example.

Speaking and peaking

A Circle speaker recently pointed out that "SPEAKING" contains the word "PEAKING."

Holly Stiel uses Speaking Circle tools to help hotels, law firms, corporations, and other organizations bring the "Spirit of Hospitality" into their businesses. The benefits of better listening and connections are clear to her clients, and Holly says that people in the "support circles" she creates are "hungry for acknowledgment and support. It's rare for people to have everyone's complete attention for 2 minutes while they talk about some part of their work in which they would like to be supported, perhaps a time when they felt demeaned, or to talk about something that really pushes their buttons."

Her work helps both her clients, and *their* clients. As her clients feel heard and supported, they are better able to hear and support the people they serve. It's difficult to give people something we don't have ourselves.

Enlightened Leadership

Doug Krug is co-author of *Enlightened Leadership: Getting to the Heart of Change*, and conducts seminars that turn managers into leaders. He believes the skills we use in Transformational Speaking are the wave of the future:

> When we go into a company, they're often afraid we'll do too much "touchy feely" stuff. We do just that, and people eat it up. At one major corporation, the "hammer guy" met me for breakfast the week after our first session and said, "My understanding is that everybody cried in there." I confirmed the report, and he said he was sorry he had missed that first session, but was looking forward to the second because he couldn't remember the last time he had cried.
>
> People just aren't getting results the old way, with all the hierarchy and posturing. They're really starting to understand that they need to be real in order to be productive. When they reach a high enough level of frustration with the old way, they're ready to try something new.
>
> In the speaking world, fewer and fewer people are willing to accept a "schtick" speaker. Transformational Speaking is a bridge to authenticity, and that's why everybody wants it. They want someone who can be real. We all know when someone is just blowing smoke.
>
> In our company, we want people presenting our programs who don't have all the answers, because our work is to help our clients find their *own* answers. We have a number of new people that we want to do Speaking Circles. There probably isn't a leader in this country who couldn't benefit from them.

Explosive listening

"Explosive Listening" is a phrase coined by Michael Gahagan, General Manager at WZTR in Milwaukee, who attended a communication workshop I conducted at the Radio Advertising Bureau convention in Dallas. After twenty years in the business, he discovered a whole new way of listening and relating to customers. Here's what happened, in Michael's words.

> We had a client who had done a lot of business with us in the past, and then suddenly stopped buying from us. We tried a couple of different ways to find out what the problem was. I went down there, we changed sales reps, but we never really felt like we were getting the whole story—so we never knew how to get back into this client's good graces. We offered some solutions, but we were presenting into a vacuum because we didn't really know what the root problem was.

> So one day I went down there and said to this individual, "Why don't you tell me a little bit about what's changed in your mind about us." He listed some of the things we'd already heard, so I just kept saying, "Okay, yes" and encouraging him to continue talking. At some point, he said, "That's about it." I didn't say anything. He just kind of looked at me, and I still didn't say anything. Really, for about 30 seconds, I just didn't say anything.

> And then he erupted! It was incredible the amount of stuff that came out of him. I think part of it was that he felt relaxed, and he felt comfortable because it was a very nonthreatening way of listening. It was just like, "I'm here, talk to me." Well, now we're going to be able to give him what he needs and not what we *think* he needs.

> That same Speaking Circle listening has helped me internally with my staff as well. Instead of telling them what I think they need, I ask them what they need. And sometimes that happens best when I just shut up and listen.

Michael now trains his sales staff not to beat down people's objections. If someone says, "I just can't afford to buy right now," they don't rush in to deny or fix the problem. Instead, they stay quiet and listen. Michael tells me that invariably, when the person feels heard, he or she virtually *explodes* with the information his people need to serve them and make the sale.

Explosive Listening is the capacity to make others feel fully heard in our presence, and it is the million-dollar communications skill. This deep listening can be applied not just to sales presentations, but to customer relations, executive training, leading meetings, employee training, team-building, one-on-one communication, management training, and morale building.

Explosive Listening, like Transformational Speaking, cannot be taught with technique. But it can be *caught* by experiencing a Speaking Circle. As a result of that Radio Advertising Bureau convention in Dallas, radio stations around the country now begin their sales team meetings with a 2-minute go-around in which everyone gets to voice concerns, acknowledgments, and wins—or just receive attention and support. Stations are finding that when people start the day being fully heard and fully seen, even for 2 minutes, they are better able to go out and allow their customers to feel fully seen and fully heard. That's what each of us craves, and it's great for the bottom line.

Explosive Listening even works in the news business. Robin Doussard, former *San Jose Mercury News* Feature Editor and current Assistant Managing Editor of the *Orange County Register*, told me about a reporter who always got incredible quotes at accident scenes. He came back to the newsroom with stuff that no one else could get, and colleagues began to suspect that he was making some of it up. Robin finally asked him what his secret was, what questions he asked. The reporter said, "I don't ask anything. I don't say anything. I just stand there and let them be, and I listen. When they feel heard, they pour their hearts out. They tell me everything. They just blurt it out."

A Circle Speaker and top sales person says, "I'm better able to listen to clients now. I'm not so quick to jump in with my stories while they're telling their stories. I breathe with them when they are talking, and I can almost see them get more comfortable when I do that. In the past, I was driven by a fear that I wasn't good enough, and that drove me to a lot of extra chatter. I don't have to try so hard to convince people now that I have more strength inside."

Customers in any business need to be fully seen and heard. For the most part, this need goes unmet. If we can meet it, we're ahead of the game. In 4 years selling houses for Coldwell Banker, the largest real estate firm in the country, Maureen Gilmartin has risen to 16th ranked agent out of 56,000 nationally. In crediting Speaking Circles for honing the connecting and listening skills that made this possible, she says, "It's helped my business tremendously, because 90% of real estate success is making potential clients feel heard."

Explosive Listening is a primary skill not just for sales people but for leaders in all areas. We get the information we need to do the job in the best way possible—no matter what the job is.

Action without resistance

Most business is about results. The way to produce results and nurture human values at the same time is to inspire action without resistance, to make producing results a rewarding, life-enhancing, inspiring process for ourselves and the people with whom we work.

People find it easier to commit to action that supports their own sense of meaning in life. When we communicate values and passions that are genuine for us, and that they share, they respond to our calls to action from a gut feeling of rightness. That's more powerful than any amount of persuasion. They are committed 100% to meeting objectives because they trust our motives and share the mission.

That kind of connection between leaders and their teams happens when the leaders speaks simply, clearly, conversationally from their own passion. Transformational Speakers often become Transformational Leaders because they are clear about their passions, and communicate them in a human way directly to the hearts of people on their teams.

Transformational "people skills"

Transformational Speakers excel at three important "people skills" in business: interviewing, training, and managing others. Here is what a few have shared about their creative application of Speaking Circle skills to their work in these areas.

- Hal Bennet of Menlo Park, California, a consultant to companies like 3M, says, "I use it not just in presentations, but in conducting meetings. If a person hasn't said anything, they're not really in the meeting—and at least half of the people in meetings don't say anything. I like to go around the room and let everyone have the group's full attention before we start, so that they're engaged from the beginning.

   "I also find that, when discussing issues, it helps to let everybody have their full say without being interrupted—and then go on to the next person. You might think that discussing things back and forth would be more productive, but I've found that when you do it so that everybody says their full say and feels heard, it actually goes more quickly and everyone feels more complete."

- Gayle Miller of Columbus, Ohio, a training and organizational development consultant, and most recently an education manager for a major bank, says, "I no longer have that intense upper body stress—tension and perspiration—when I am in front of a group, or on a business call or job interview. I breathe, slow my pace, look people in the eye, and am myself. In a training session I led after 5 months of Speaking Circle involvement, I followed a university president who spoke *at* the group for 90 minutes. When I started, I paused, breathed, and connected. The group responded, interacted with me throughout the 3 hours I had—and gave me big applause."

- Robin Blanc of Colorado Springs is a corporate trainer and coach in the areas of leadership, high performance and career transition who says, "After people have lost their jobs, they are very vulnerable, scared, and often in pain. As I utilize the principles of Speaking Circles, the trust appears to develop quicker and the clients seem more open and receptive."

- Becca Kozlowski, an account executive and trainer with Clarke American in Columbus, Ohio, says, "I no longer spend all my preparation time rehearsing what I am going to say and where I am going to stand. That leaves me time to find out about the real people in my audience and what their needs are. So when I do get up in front of a group I no longer am acting but communicating, even when I'm the only one speaking. Speaking Circles have made me feel more confident in both the selling and training arena."

Better than free publicity

Transformational Speaking is good for business in another unexpected way. It gives us the skills to speak about our product or
service in public, and perhaps even get paid for doing so. The
only thing better than free publicity is publicity for which *they pay
us!*

American businesses and associations hold a million meetings
a year. That's 3,000 a day. There is no shortage of audiences in
our country. Service clubs, Chambers of Commerce, business
brown bag luncheons, community and church groups are always
looking for speakers to do talks. Many of these engagements are
"gratis," but some are not. People who give others a powerful
experience of their presence as they talk about the benefits of what
they do can get paid to promote their businesses.

Even if we speak for free, these kinds of meetings provide a
limitless source of free publicity, great word of mouth, and dynamic networking—as well as opportunities to practice our presence in front of the room.

Unlimited potential

There are thousands of ways to use the skills of Transformational
Speaking in business. Here are a few that Circle Speakers are cur-
rently using to create opportunities.

New kinds of marketing.
A stockbroker now invites groups of clients to lunch talks on
various investment subjects, and those clients bring their friends.

Transformational phoning.
The phone is the perfect vehicle for listening. A star sales person says, "This process has revolutionized my style on sales calls.
I'm much more relaxed now, and find I can often make that silent
connection even without eye contact. I have slowed down to listen differently than before, and even add more humor to my phone
presentations."

New careers.

Many people find that feeling comfortable with speaking and communicating opens up possibilities they hadn't even considered before. "I have become a tour guide since attending a Speaking Circle and had no difficulty speaking to the busload of travelers and being myself and having fun with them. The Speaking Circle helped me accept myself and be comfortable with myself before a group. I don't have to be someone I'm not ever again!"

Personal depth in impersonal fields.

A trial attorney says:

> I was tired of having only impersonal, adversarial relationships with people. I wanted to win cases, but that doesn't have to mean treating people like objects. I find now I can argue the case, but talk to juries, my opponents, and judges like real people. I was hesitant at first because I thought it might make me lose my edge, but my guess is it's actually helped my work. Also, I don't feel so schizophrenic when I leave the courtroom. I can go back into my personal life and be the same person I was all day.

Good clean fun.

Many already successful people find that The Laughing Spirit restores fun to work that had become almost rote. A corporate trainer says, "I've done hundreds and hundreds of presentations, very well, but this work taught me to bring in some humor, and also to wait until I found my speech waiting for me in the audience. It's an adventure now, a challenge, and it hasn't been that way for a long time."

Soul.

A nurse and trainer shares, "I've been trying to teach 'presence' to health professionals across the country because health care is so *hurried*. I tell them you can go quickly, but not be in a hurry. And when you go quickly, it's still possible to *be in the room* with people. Patients always know when you're 'there,' and when you're not. They know if you're not really paying attention to them, and when you're more interested in their tubes, numbers, or blood work—and not looking at them as a whole."

Think about the ways you could use Transformational Speaking to enhance, upgrade, or enjoy your work more. In the next chapter, we'll look at some of the ways this kind of speaking makes life *away* from the platform richer. ◎

Chapter 13

Growing into Ourselves: Speaking as Transformation

Many people come to Speaking Circles specifically to grow psychologically, emotionally, and spiritually. Others come to enhance their careers or improve their presentation, and are amazed that they also experience great personal growth.

Change, growth, and personal evolution are inevitable results of Transformational Speaking because we focus on being present, authentic, open, and connected with ourselves and others.

Today, this kind of inner work, sensitivity, and ability to listen are essential not just for quality relationships, but in almost every kind of work.

Finishing old business

Personal transformation always involves finishing old business and healing old wounds. These old resentments and frustrations fall away naturally in Speaking Circles.

The healing takes place on two fronts:

1. *As we speak about painful incidents from the past, we begin to forgive and heal them.*

Although there is no need or instruction to speak of these past hurts, they often emerge as people go deeper within themselves. As we bring them into the light, rather than keeping them hidden and festering within us, they lose their emotional charge. Their power over us starts to dissipate. In this process, we also come to a better understanding of how other people's pasts affect their behavior, and how we all react to one another.

2. *The support we receive from the group is healing, in and of itself.*

In the light, love, and support of a Speaking Circle, past injuries and hurts we didn't even know we had are washed away.

Here are a few ways that people have experienced this healing.

- A therapist told me, "In just a few months of doing Circles, I can remember incidents from twenty or thirty years ago that I'm now using to work with my clients. I had completely blocked a lot of those memories, but now I can even remember people's names, what the rooms looked like, what plants and pictures were there—it's like television. Some of those situations were so conflicted, and now I'm working them out. I'm amazed at the enormous healing power of this process."

- "Now I see those bad memories as precious. They're little teachings, entertainments, gifts that have brought me to where I am today," says another Speaker.

- "I talk about things to get clear on them. I'll tell a story that still has some charge, and see how it comes out this time. Eventually, the charge will disappear, and telling about some huge incident will be like talking about a trip to the grocery store. If there's a challenge or problem or obstacle I'm facing, I talk about it in the Circle and the answers just come."

- "The Speaking Circles are great at 'restructuring' my family patterns. That time is purely, intimately mine—and that makes me want to give the same thing to others. I've become more connected throughout my life, and I found a voice inside me I didn't know I had."
- "No matter how terrible I feel before I Circle, I go and just tell the truth about where I am. When I do that, the energy blows off. If I start from where I really am, I always move."

David Roche talks about how he handled a facial disfigurement that he had never talked about openly before his Speaking Circle.

> I lived with a lot of denial, so this was the window to look at myself as I really am. In my family, we dealt with it by not talking about it. Talking about it was part of making me whole.
>
> The experience of being disfigured and being on-stage taught me that people are afraid because of the fears it raises in them about themselves. Everybody feels disfigured in some way. It's part of human experience to worry about whether we are acceptable. Now I understand that, and I can talk about my face.

David has transformed his disfigurement into a one-man show which recently opened in San Francisco to rave reviews and sold-out theaters.

Sometimes Circle Speakers can prevent other people's "old business" from getting started in the first place. Hypnotherapist and Circle facilitator Cathy Dana says, "Once when I was substituting for a first grade teacher, one of the little girls had scribbled all over her page instead of coloring within the lines. Everyone was laughing at her, so I picked up her paper and said, 'Oh, what beautiful colors!' The laughter quieted down and she immediately brightened up. I felt like the guardian of her creative spirit, without making the others wrong."

Accepting and loving ourselves

The whole point of healing the past and letting go of old business
is to accept and love ourselves. That is the cornerstone of all growth
and self-expression—and the foundation of Transformational
Speaking.

When we see ourselves reflected in the audience's eyes, we know
that we are someone, and that we are okay. When we fully embrace ourselves where we are, we can go forward and become even
more of ourselves in all areas of life: family, work, art, friendships,
spirituality, business, etc.

The guru here is the structure of the Speaking Circle—and that's
accessible to everyone, all over the world, at no cost whatsoever.
We can give that to one another for free.

Knowing ourselves and finding our message

Whatever our journey, Transformational Speaking fuels the quest.
"I'm on a hero's journey out there in the world—going to Antarc-
tica, being a firefighter, building a business, fighting battles," says
one man. "Transformational Speaking is an inner journey."

Another Speaker says, "I teach myself every time I talk. For the
past 3 years, I've done nothing but change. I've been like a snake
shedding my skin. Each week in class, I shed more and more of
that skin. I see what I want to keep and what I want to throw
away."

Taking the Circle home

One of the biggest Speaking Circle payoffs is the ability to communicate more clearly and cleanly with family, friends, and other personal relationships—and still keep our warm connections with these people. Transformational Speaking is just as useful around the dinner table as it is around the conference table or in an auditorium.

"I had dinner with my ex-husband, the second time I've seen him in 25 years," says a Circle Speaker. "I'd never felt heard by him, and for the first time I wasn't concerned about that. Instead, I assumed I would be heard and made sure to take as much time as I needed to get my ideas out. I was no longer the passive, supportive one who only spoke when I was given permission. I knew I had a right to be heard, and I could also listen openly without feeling the need to comment on everything he said. The other new thing was that I *expected* to be supported. Once I'd had that deep experience of being supported by others in Circle, I've carried the feeling with me. And it spreads to others."

We take ourselves with us wherever we go. Once we've mastered the skills of Transformational Speaking in one area, we have them everywhere.

Jump-starting creativity

People often say that being in Speaking Circles enhances their creativity—regardless of whether they are involved in speaking, writing, art, music, human relations, business, or some other form of expression. I believe that Transformational Speaking actually jumpstarts something that happens *before* creativity. I call it *"expressivity."*

Expressivity is the raw, essential, vital energy that we use our creativity to mold into various forms of expression: painting, music, writing, relationships, playing, public speaking, etc. It is that explosive, unformed energy that comes *just before* creativity—the inspiration that made Mozart or Shakespeare pick up their pens.

Each of us has our own unique brand or frequency of expressivity. To discover and tap into that creative power, we need a safe place. We need to be able to stand before ourselves and others in an open, vulnerable way and let whatever is within us bubble up or burst forth. We can't try to control it, or know how it's going to turn out. We just have to let whatever is there spew forth.

That means we need permission to make "mistakes." We'll never touch that raw energy if we have to be perfect. We have to allow for the rough draft, the wrong note, the talk that doesn't quite ring true but is accepted and supported anyway. If we don't have permission to do it "wrong," we never let it rip. And if we can't let it rip, we can't get to expressivity.

In music classes, nobody expects that students will sit down and immediately play perfect pieces. They practice, make mistakes, and nobody says, "OOHH, that's awful!" We know they're just practicing, so they can get better and play their hearts out. But when it comes to speaking or communicating, we sometimes demand perfection. Speaking Circles give us permission to blow the wrong notes occasionally without cutting us off at the knees and stopping the flow of expressivity. We get to be ourselves and tell our truth without being concerned about how we look.

The great thing about expressivity in that once we tap into it in one form, like Speaking Circles, we have access to it in all other forms of expression. When we know where to go to get that energy when we speak, we can also find it when we write, sing, act, sculpt, socialize, or put together a creative business deal. Many writers find their voice as speakers, and take it back to the written word. They say their work is more authentic, and much stronger, after they've tapped into their expressivity as speakers.

"Speaking Circles took me down into the raw essence of myself," said one writer. "It was like a geyser."

In a sense, expressivity is our life force. That's why this process has such broad application. When we unleash that life force, it touches everything we do.

Where no Circle has gone before

When we find a safe, fun environment in which we grow and expand, we naturally want to share it with others. Speaking Circles have become part of many professional settings, communities, spiritual organizations, and other groups because Transformational Speakers have brought them there.

Any culture—business, family, relationship, church, community organization, or support groups already organized around certain issues—can adopt the Speaking Circle principles of receiving, connection, authenticity, and listening. Most groups immediately become more nurturing, exciting, expansive, and productive when these principles become part of the culture.

"I have a safe, loving place where each week I can stop, be seen, drop down into myself and tell total truth," says one minister. "I can peel off my skin and let the light of my Circle shine within me. It's easier for me to go into new experiences, accept gifts and opportunities offered to me, and have fun, because I no longer think everyone is judging me."

In the past few years, Transformational Speakers have started Circles for teens, elders, prison inmates, people with AIDS, cancer patients, health professionals, and other special groups. Here is what some of them have said.

- Lauren Britt is a clinical social worker who trains social work interns to work with children and families. She began a Circle for inner city public school sixth graders, and says, "It's just very simple and straightforward, and it works for youths for that reason. Young people aren't used to getting that much positive attention, so they go for the negative because they do want attention. They like this process; they're into it. They are talking about things that are meaningful to them: racism, violence, and difficult family situations."

- Hair stylist Rebecca Beardsley started a Circle in her salon. "It's a natural place for a Circle, because there's a lot of sharing your stories and expressing yourself from a natural place. I feel like there's a fuller self that's playing now, that Circles have opened up a whole new part of me."

- "I belong to a men's group and we used this method in the group," says a musician. "This style of speaking is like ancient wisdom. We get away from debate and arguing, and just express our personal truth. As we each express our truth, we build the kind of community the world needs."

- "I wish I'd known about positive feedback when I was raising children. And coaching Little League!" says a personnel manager. "I used to say, 'Don't drop your right arm.' Now I would say, 'Keep your right arm up.'"

Speaking as meditation

When we stand before the audience and receive their support, the feelings of connection and love that rush through us usually stop the mental chatter. We are swept up into a peaceful, serene, yet energetic state very similar to what meditators describe.

We speak from a place of stillness, from the calm, loving presence of our hearts. We explore the intuitive voice that is always present, but often hidden from our conscious mind. We happen on inner Truths just waiting to be discovered. We connect with our spiritual selves, and find out how much we actually know when we are willing to move beyond the limitations of space and time.

Transformational Speakers have told me for years that they use speaking as a meditation:

- "Being present fully in the moment—here and now, as speaker or listener—is vital to a soulful life. Speaking Circles have been a major force of light in my transformation process this year."
- "The most important things for me are love, being genuine, and enjoying the support of the group. It was almost a mystical feeling. It proves that we have abilities and functions that we didn't know existed."
- "I've been a mediator for twenty years and call the circle I lead 'Speaking as Meditation.' To speak from our Truth, we have to come from a place of inner silence. Slowing everything down lets us listen to our own voices. As we do that, we begin to understand the deeper connection we have to spirit or the whole."
- "It's become part of my spiritual practice, the practice of presence."
- "It's all about naturalness, mindfulness, stillness, and listening while speaking."

Ann Weiser Cornell, teacher of the Focusing Process, shared how Speaking Circles helped her develop her speeches and her new book, *The Power of Focusing: A Practical Guide to Emotional Self-Healing* (New Harbinger, 1996):

> In the Circles, I just started coming out more and more to speak my truth, rather than talking about some vague, general topic that I thought other people would be interested in. Each week, I told more of my own heart—and learned how to tell stories, personal stories from my own life that helped people have an experience of what I was saying. By the time I gave my first big talk, I knew what I wanted to say. My book is coming out this year, and I feel so much more ready to talk to people about it.

In the next few chapters, we will explore how to put your own talk together and take it out into the world. ◎

Chapter 14

So You're Going to Give a Talk

Imagine that you've put together your own Speaking Circle and have been practicing Transformational Speaking for a while. You've begun to find your Truth and your voice, and each week you're getting a stronger sense that you have a message to deliver.

You know this message would enhance people's lives, and you've even begun to envision spreading your wings and speaking about it in public. You don't know exactly how to get started, but you're about ready to do *something*.

Suddenly, out of the blue, your church or community group calls and asks you to give a presentation at their next meeting. What do you do?

This chapter covers the basics of getting ready for a talk—both internally, and on the podium.

Preparing from the inside out

Speaking is one of the most powerful ways we can contribute to life, and we need to honor that in ourselves.

Adopt the attitude that you are a shining light, sent into the world to deliver this specific message. If people didn't need to hear it, you wouldn't be moved to share it.

You're not telling people "how it is" or shoving your point of view down their throats. You're simply sharing your own experience, giving them your unique perspective on a situation in which you've met a challenge, and offering it in the hope that they will find it as useful as you have.

I worked with Lency Spezzano, a healer in Hawaii, to find her message and develop her talk. Lency remembered being a little girl who was very happy and talked to birds and cats and flowers. When she was 5, she tried to help her mother out of a depression by saying, "Mom, the world is an incredibly wonderful place. Life is just a miracle."

Her mother looked at her and said, "No, Lency, life is a struggle. You don't get to be happy till you die and go to heaven." With those words, Lency fell into a dark downward spiral of depression that lasted for many years. It took a long time and a lot of work to pull herself out of that spiral and see the light again. But today, Lency's talk is about moving from darkness into light. She is still in the tunnel sometimes, but she sees the light at its end and is a little ahead of other people. She shines her light for others so that they can keep moving.

This is all any of us can do. We can shine the light of our own experience on a situation, and hope that others are helped. We can't save them or make them move—but we can show them where our light is shining.

A writer and professional speaker once told me:

> When the talk becomes so big that it's just making itself known through me, and I become just the vehicle for the talk, the power of the truth takes over. Service comes out of our intimacy with the audience, and becoming whatever

we're talking about. They live within whatever that is for a while and have an experience of it because they're connected to us.

Knowing what to say

Many of us know instinctively that we have something to say, but need to spend some time focusing in on exactly what our message is and how best to deliver it.

Clients often tell me, "I know I have something to give, but I don't know how to frame it. I don't know how to put myself forward." It's as if little Speaking Angels are sitting on their shoulders, nudging them to get out there even before they are 100% clear about what they want to say. Those angels are delivering the message: "It's time to get clear. If not now, when?"

The first thing I tell people is that we know more than we think we know about our message. It's just a matter of sitting down and figuring out what we *do* know.

Many people begin this process by picturing themselves standing behind a dark oak lectern in front of a large group of people— usually very judgmental, easily bored, critical people who have gathered to decide whether the speaker has any value as a purveyor of information or as a human being.

This is not a good place to start. Instead, sit down with a trusted friend or coach, and perhaps a tablet of paper, and ask yourself what you know about life. Here are some questions that might prompt ideas:

- What has life taught you?
- What have been the turning points in your life? In what directions have you turned at these points? What have you learned?
- What secrets have you discovered?
- Who are the people who inspired you in your life?
- When you comfort or counsel friends, what do you usually wind up talking about?

- Into which areas of life do you have particularly clear insight?
- What are you good at?
- Where do you seem to have a unique perspective?
- What obstacles have you overcome? What did you use to overcome them?

Brick walls that become teachers

Your message probably has something to do with obstacles, weaknesses, fears, failures, or limitations that you have overcome. You may have found a way through the problem that other people can use to get through similar problems, or through problems that are the same but not as extreme.

For instance, I know a businessman who has such severe dyslexia that he reads at the 4th-grade level, and yet he is extremely successful and very wealthy. He is in great demand as a speaker, and travels around the country talking about how to deal with learning disabilities. People are inspired by his life, and how he overcame his limitation. He sees his dyslexia as a gift, because it forced him to become a bigger person—and, in the end, it gave him his vehicle for expressing himself and serving people.

Our situations don't have to be as dramatic as the dyslexic businessman's. We find unique ways to overcome life's smaller difficulties every day.

Quite often, we use our greatest strength to overcome our greatest limitation. We take something at which we are intuitively brilliant, and apply it to our weakness. For example, my limitation was that I couldn't be heard. As the youngest in my family, I was never heard or credited with much—and this pattern carried over into my adult life. The backward, wounded part of me was nervousness, fear, and confusion about expressing myself. My great strength was that I had a deep, instinctive grasp of group dynamics. I could tell exactly what was going on in any group, without thinking about it.

As I started teaching and coaching, I began to apply my greatest strength to my greatest weakness. I experimented with using group support to encourage clearer, more connected communication and expression. As I did that, I saw that *my problem was a universal problem.* A lot of people felt nervous and confused about expressing themselves—and it turned out that group support was an almost universal solution. Speaking Circles are the result of using my greatest strength to overcome my greatest obstacle.

When we have that chemistry, bringing the greatest strength and greatest weakness together to solve the problem, then we have something to teach others. The next step is putting it out there. I could have packed up and said, "Well, *my* problem's solved. I'm going home." Letting people know about it, putting together a talk to promote it, and being willing to do Circles for only a few people at first were the first steps in bringing Transformational Speaking out into the world.

We can also find our message by looking at turning points in our lives.

Turning points

Sometimes our message grows out of turning points that change the direction of our lives: a divorce, a marriage, the birth of a child, a death or illness, meeting a significant teacher, getting fired, moving to a new city, a career change, joining a spiritual group, getting a certain degree. Turning points are marked by crisis, opportunity, failure, and/or inspiration.

Often, these events determine what we do with our lives, and make us the people we are today. We can usually trace our passions and commitments back to them—or to the people involved in them. These formative experiences contain the roots of our passion, and our message comes from our passion.

We all know of people who found their message and their life's work in turning points. Candy Lightner founded MADD (Mothers Against Drunk Driving) after her child was killed by a drunk driver. Basketball's Magic Johnson began his work on behalf of people with HIV after he contracted the condition.

Sometimes we're reluctant to discuss these turning points in public because they seem too personal, or we don't trust our abil ity to tell them well, or we're not sure what point they make, or we just don't seem to remember the right ones. *Telling the meaning of a turning point experience can take as little as a minute.* It can be very simple, and it is an extraordinarily effective tool—both for finding your message and for delivering it.

Big small moments

Our messages can also come out of smaller, quieter moments.

I once worked with the owner of a very successful employment agency who had been asked to give a talk and didn't know what to say. I asked her what was going on in her life, and to describe a few incidents that had happened in the last few weeks.

She told the story of walking her daughter to her first day at kindergarten, and the little girl saying, "Mommy, you're squeezing my hand too tight!" I asked her how that might apply to her business, and she suddenly realized that she had been squeezing her managers too tightly. Then I asked her what would happen if she went in and told her managers that story. That woman could easily develop a professional talk called "Hands-Off Management" on promoting high self-esteem and self-direction among managers, letting go of the need to control, and trusting managers to do a good job.

Another client was an antique specialist who wanted to start a speaking career. Her parents had been antique dealers and she'd known everything about this field since she was a child—but she couldn't quite find the particular slant, hook, or angle she wanted to use. I knew what she did, but I kept asking her, "What do you do?" Each time, her answer got shorter. And each time, I asked her to tell me more succinctly what she did.

Finally, she said in frustration, "I feel like I was born in an antique shop!" That became the first sentence of her talk. It piqued people's interest and was the perfect lead for the kind of personal, intimate, cozy chat she liked to have with groups about antiques and the antique business.

Imagine your audience

Earlier I said that most people start by imagining a critical, easily bored audience—and many of them get so intimidated they never find their message. Instead, imagine yourself before a small, supportive group of people who really want to hear what you have to say.

What would be the first thing you'd say to this group? What do you want them to know about you? You may find your message there. If nothing comes to mind, just keep standing there, patient and relaxed. If you wait long enough for those first words, you'll probably have your lead sentence. If you just keep standing there in your imagination and coming up with things you want to tell them, you'll discover many of the elements of your talk.

Next, think about your through-line and title. What is the one thing you want them to get? What point of view do you want to impart to them? Your whole talk will be built around making sure these points get delivered.

Then you can start thinking about your opening, and begin to structure your talk. We'll deal with the opening and structure in the next two chapters.

That's how you find your message and create your talk out of nothing.

"Do"s and "Don't"s

For your first talk, here are some basic reminders before you walk to the platform.

DO:

- Silently receive your listeners for at least a few seconds before you speak.
- Speak only to individuals, lingering with each person for 5 to 10 seconds before moving on.

- Speak in short sentences, pausing frequently to connect with individuals.

- Leave longer silences between important points to let your words sink in and to give your listeners a chance to digest the information.
- Stand relatively still and move slightly *toward* individuals as you speak to them.
- Use relaxing humor based on your own experiences, if you use humor at all.
- Stand still and receive your applause at the end of your talk. Take it into your heart.

DON'T:

- Start talking immediately to cover up anxiety or project "confidence."
- Speak to "the group" as a whole, darting or scanning your eyes to make surface eye contact for 1 to 2 seconds with many people.
- Connect your sentences with "and" or "so," and pull away from eye contact in transition between points.
- Cover up natural silences with "um"s and "ah"s, rush to the next point to avoid "dead air," or switch your attention inward to prepare the next sentence.
- Pace from side to side to "cover the audience," while making staged gestures.

- Tell jokes, or be clever, quick, glib, offhand, or cute.

- Walk off "modestly" as you are being applauded.

You have to start somewhere

You've found your message and used the next few chapters to prepare your talk. Now what? Where do you start?

Remember that community groups, professional associations, and service clubs are constantly open to speakers to "entertain the troops" for a half hour to an hour at no cost. Local libraries and phone books have lists of these groups. Simply call the number, ask to speak to the program chairman, and tell him or her about your talk. Take advantage of speaking opportunities at your church, school, hospital, or neighborhood groups as well. The more practice you get, the better you become.

Many very successful speakers started out this way. As you gain experience and contacts, you can start charging money and speaking to larger groups.

If professional speaking interests you, look into joining a local chapter of the National Speakers Association. NSA has been my professional association since 1989 and its members are typically supportive and resourceful live wires. Call (602) 968-2552 for information.

And don't be afraid to bomb. I bombed horribly on my first professional speaking engagement—and lived not only to tell the tale, but to become a professional speaking coach.

In the next two chapters, we'll start putting together the nuts and bolts of your talk. We'll begin with the perfect opening, and move through all three parts of your talk to the climactic end. ◎

Chapter 15

The Perfect Opening

On September 13, 1991, Mario Cuomo, then Governor of New York and perennial non-candidate for President, stood before a frigid audience at the convention of the National Association of Broadcasters.

But as he told stories of his boyhood and his relationship with his mother, warm smiles spread through the room. Cuomo worked his magic in an easy, conversational way, with pauses to listen as his words sunk into the broadcasters' hearts. At the end of his talk, he got a standing ovation—not by pumping up his audience, but by telling personal stories in a quiet conversational style.

The *San Francisco Chronicle* ended its report on the event with, "Although the broadcasters initially appeared to be cool to Cuomo, they warmed to him as he told stories of his youth and of his mother, who speaks to him in Italian."

We can learn two things from Cuomo's winning over this hardened, sophisticated group of broadcasters:

- Opening a talk with a personal story that makes us vulnerable and has universal application is a powerful way to compel rapt and instant attention.
- This only works when we are genuinely connected with both our story and the individuals in the audience. We can't fake it. People know when they are being emotionally manipulated.

The quality of attention that an audience gives us is usually determined in the first 5 minutes. This chapter is about the most effective way to open your talk, what you must include to keep the audience's attention, and how to bring people to the edge of their seats.

The choice between you, and Tahiti

When you first stand before a group, what you have in front of you is basically a disorganized collection of individuals. Most audiences are fragmented in two ways.

First, they aren't particularly connected with one another.

Second, each individual's attention is split in several different directions. They're thinking about a disagreement with a co-worker, their kid's report card, lunch, various flickering unconscious doubts or fears about the day or year, resentment about the bad conversation at dinner last night, sex, their financial situation, wouldn't it be better just to be lying on a beach in Tahiti, and a variety of other human concerns. Many of these things are calling to them just as loudly as you are.

Most listeners are not consciously aware of these subtle dynamics. Nor do most speakers know that this is the game they are playing each time they step to the front. But the truth is, you have 5 minutes to get your show on the road.

There are two sure-fire ways to grab our audience's attention, put them at ease, and shape them into a community:

1. *The personal, universal story*
2. *Answering every audience's four burning questions.*

Your personal, universal story

Mario Cuomo warmed up a cold audience with a personal story that had universal applications. Every broadcaster in the room had some warm childhood memories, and they were triggered as Cuomo relived his. Like Cuomo, we can connect with our audience by sharing stories that are real and unique to us, but also so universal that everyone has his or her own version of them and feels immediate empathy with us.

The personal, universal story—related in a conversational, emotionally open style in 3 minutes or less—makes us one with our audience. It compels rapt attention by breaking the illusion of separation and bonding us as a group. We are all grounded in our common humanity. While we are telling our story, the audience members are finding their own similar stories. They know that we are as vulnerable as they are, and that we are here as one of them.

We can say "hello" to an individual by simply looking into his or her eyes and saying, "Hello." But to bond a group of people to us, and to one another, we have to tell a story to which everyone can relate. We let everyone sit back, remembering a similar emotional experience. In this way, we form the group into a community.

I believe that there is a perfect opening for every audience. Recently I spoke to the American Association of Medical Transcriptionists, and got their attention with this opening:

"In 1970 I was diagnosed with testicular melanoma, and had a transperitonial lymph node dissection.

"I'm telling you this for two reasons. One, this is the first audience I've ever spoken to who would understand just what I meant. [Laughter] And secondly, when I researched what you folks do, I realized that there must have been a medical transcriptionist involved in my successful treatment, but that the nature of this work keeps you in the background. So this is the first chance I've had to say thank you."

When I left a long pause for my gratitude to sink in, a chorus spontaneously formed and shouted, "You're welcome!"

"Now," I said after another pause, "what can I do for *you*?" We were completely connected, and that opening started a wonderful day.

We may deliver our personal, universal story in a casual, conversational style—but we remember that it has a job to do. It has to put our audience *at ease with us, and with one another*. It has to bring us all together into a community.

Our story is only one part of a great opening. We must also answer the four burning questions on every audience's mind, so that they can relax and get comfortable with us.

The four burning questions

The four burning questions on every audience's mind are:

1. Who are you?

The personal, universal story answers this question by humanizing us, making us vulnerable, connecting us to them and to each other, showing them what makes us tick.

Remember to pause, receive their support, and make eye contact with one person before speaking your opening line: "Peoria, 1995. I was lying flat in a dentist's chair, bright lights shining in my eyes, people in surgical masks hovering above me..." Then pause again for a few seconds while the whole audience joins you in that time and place. Presto! You have created community.

2. Why are you here?

This is the logical conclusion to your personal story. What did you learn? What is the moral of the story? What about that story, when you follow the thread, brings you here today in all your passion to give them your message? "When I learned so tragically that no one need lose their teeth if they floss every day, I made it my life's work to get the word out."

3. What are we going to do?

Review your agenda for the talk in no more than three sentences. Tell them what you are going to tell them. "So today I will discuss the myths about plaque. I'll tell you about the truly scandalous nature of strep, and then I'll share the five secrets of flossing effectively."

4. What's in it for me?

Promise them a specific benefit. "By the time I'm done, you will see that flossing is fun and financially rewarding, and you'll never again leave home without it!"

With that flourish, pause to gather their agreement that they are in the right place and ready to come along with you. To do this, you can use phrases like:

- "Would this be useful to you?"
- "Are you in the right place?"
- "Any questions?"

It's easy to create your opening following this simple format.

Seven steps to the perfect opening

Here is another way to look at presenting the perfect opening. It includes steps for connecting with your audience, as well as for telling your personal, universal story and answering the four burning questions. These seven steps are:

1. Your nonverbal opening.

When the applause ends, we have a tendency to start talking immediately. Instead, honor the silence for at least 5 to 10 seconds. Center yourself and breathe. You may want to close your eyes for a moment or gently flex your knees. Take in the entire room, then individual faces. Feel the goodwill for you out there. The foundation of our authentically supportive relationship with the audience is laid *before we say a word*. Resist the urge to send out an ingratiating smile that begs, "Please like me." Don't speak until you make true eye contact with one individual beaming at you. Say your first sentence directly *to that person*.

2. Your opening line.

Resist the temptation to open with a nicety, such as, "It's great to be here," or "Thank you, Maureen, for that wonderful introduction." Instead, thank your introducer personally as he or she leaves the stage and concentrate on the audience once you arrive at the podium.

Unless you are an accomplished humorist, it's rarely a good idea to open with a joke. The rewards are minimal and the risks are great.

Your opening line should bring listeners right into your personal, universal story. Make it short, and make it something that *transports them directly to a specific time, place, and situation.* Some examples:

- "Kansas City, Missouri. 1980. I got fired."
- "When I graduated from college, I knew everything."
- "Got a call from my mom last night." (Only if you really did get that call.)

When everybody travels with you to that point in time and space, you all have a common meeting ground and become a community. Pause to let them gather around you.

3. The rest of your personal universal story.

Don't just recite it, but don't force feelings on the audience by overdramatizing it. Tell the story clearly and with some emotional content, but let the audience have *their own* feelings. *Relive* this turning point in your life. It might involve a failure or limitation, an obstacle in your path, perhaps an episode featuring a person who influenced your life. The rest of your story should take no more than 3 minutes. You may expand on the story in the body of your talk, but here in the opening, you are giving the headline version.

4. Transition to the present.

In no more than three sentences, connect that story, and what you learned from it, to why you are here today to talk with them about your topic.

5. *Brief agenda.*

Outline the major points you will cover in three or four concise headline sentences.

6. *Your promise.*

In one sentence, make the most provocative promise you can comfortably guarantee. This is your contract with them, and you intend to deliver on it. I worked with one woman whose promise is, "And when I am done today, you will know exactly how to reverse the aging process." And she delivers! End this sentence with a flourish, if this is comfortable for you—as if you were ending a talk.

7. *Collecting agreement.*

At this point, you will probably be facing a sea of faces nodding, "Yes, yes, yes. We are with you!" In silence, survey the audience to collect their agreement that they are in the right room and ready to take off with you. Some speakers verbalize this step with phrases like, "Okay?" "Are you ready?" "Will this be helpful?"

This is the end of the beginning. Your opening is actually a mini-talk, separate from the body of your talk. Gathering the agreement of your audience gives it closure, and signals that you are moving on to the talk itself.

The "Rapt Attention" opening

Let's look at how these principles might work in an actual opening. Since this book is about Transformational Speaking and Speaking Circles, I'll give you an opening that I might use to introduce this work. The name of this talk is "How To Compel Rapt Attention Every Time You Speak," and here is my opening.

One of the first talks I ever gave was to a Veterans' Administration program for elderly women caring for their disabled husbands—and my subject was laughter.

The presenters just before me were two nurses who demonstrated how to transfer a completely paralyzed patient from a bed to a wheelchair. Serious business. Suddenly, I heard myself being introduced to talk about humor.

As I walked to the podium, I fretted, "What can I possibly say to these women about laughter, given their dire circumstances?" As I stood before a sea of faces that looked as if they hadn't cracked a smile in years, I decided not to launch immediately into my talk. Instead, I asked in hopeful desperation, "Do any of you have examples of how you have used humor to cope with your situation?"

A 70-year-old woman named Catherine shot up her hand. She stood up and said, "My husband and I have always laughed a lot, and we still do. He has Alzheimer's Disease. Every morning he sort of forgets who I am and proposes marriage. I love it. We laugh and laugh."

One by one, the women shared their poignant, funny experiences. The theme was clear: only with laughter could they survive. I haven't spoken to a more cheerful, inspirational group since.

I have told a personal, universal story that opens a window on my world and answers question #1, "Who are you?"

What I learned from that experience was that any audience is potentially funnier than any speaker. I've expanded that realization to include the fact that every audience is a treasure trove of experience and wisdom that no speaker can match.

The depth of humanity represented in any audience will surface to the exact extent that the speaker puts a priority on the *relationship* with that audience, instead of on trying to impress them.

I'm here today to show you how to bring out the best in every group you face, so that they will bring out the best in *you*—whether you are doing an interactive program or a straight talk.

These last three sentences answer question #2, "Why are you here?"

I will first discuss the true nature of the speaker-audience relationship, and how it has been misunderstood. I will show you how to use this new understanding to open every talk in natural rapport that compels rapt attention from the first moment to the last.

Then I will provide you with a set of lifetime tools for developing audience rapport in your own natural style. You will understand why I say "There's no technique like no technique."

We now know the answer to question #3, "What are we going to do?"

When our time together today is over, you will understand exactly what it takes for you to be irresistible to audiences, without putting on a performance.

This answers question #4, "What's in it for me?"

Does this sound like something that would be valuable to you?

The "Journey to Leadership" opening

Here is the opening that my friend, professional speaker Tony Pistilli, uses for his talk on "The Journey to Leadership." See if you can follow along as he tells a story and answers the four burning questions.

For 10 years between the ages of 11 and 21, I worked full-time in a little corner grocery store in Staten Island, New York. The man I worked for eventually became my father-in-law.

As I made my deliveries, walked to school, or played with friends, I would always stop and look up whenever I heard an airplane. My parents tell me I was pointing up at airplanes from the carriage. As I looked up, I would always wonder, *"What makes them stay up?"*

Years later, I chose a career in Aerospace Engineering and Business. I studied for 8 years to find out the answer to that question, and learned all the technical and administrative skills needed to launch an 860,000-pound 747-400 aircraft carrying 420 passengers safely to their destination. Later, I became Director of Maintenance Programs for a major airline, leading a department of 250 people, overseeing a fleet of 550 aircraft making over 2,400 flights a day.

I never dreamed that the real answer to my question, *"What makes them stay up?"* was something I had learned at the littler corner grocery store—and that these skills could not be found in any textbook.

In the business, we like to think of an aircraft as 10 million parts flying in formation, but what I discovered is that a business flies only when the leader thoroughly understands relationships among people. To succeed, we need leaders. To lead, we need to know about relationships.

In a moment I will tell you the three most common misperceptions about leadership that lead to business failure. Then I will pinpoint a crossroads in my career when I was facing defeat because I believed those misperceptions. And I'll let you know how the lessons I learned about relationship in that corner grocery store got me back on track.

I will leave you with a set of tools for staying on track as successful leaders who put a priority on relationships both with associates and with customers. You will know what it takes to lead yourself and others, and to keep your aircraft in the air through all kinds of weather and turbulence, maintenance and air traffic delays, lost baggage and denied boardings.

Can you identify the various parts of this exquisite opening?

Blasting off

Opening a talk is a little like launching a spacecraft. Before you can take off, you need to gather everybody on the launching pad. To do that, you need to go around in a van and pick people up where they live.

That's what you do with your 5-minute opening. You connect them with you and with one another through your personal, universal story. You answer with crystal clarity the four questions on everybody's mind. You get their agreement that they want what you're offering, and you create community and empathy. Now you're ready to go.

In the next chapter, we answer the question, "What next?" ◎

Chapter 16

How to Structure a Talk that Gets Results

This chapter is about structuring your talk so that it reaches the most people, in the most powerful way. The structure isn't meant to limit or stifle your creativity, but to make it easier for you to communicate, and easier for the audience to hear you.

Four-part harmony: the basic parts of a successful talk

Most great talks have four parts.

You already know about one of them, the opening. In those first 5 minutes, you ground and connect the audience by reliving a concise version of your personal, universal story and answering the four burning questions: Who are you? Why are you here? What are we going to do? What's in it for me? Then you're ready for blast-off, but where do you go next?

You blast off the way every shuttle mission does—into a beautiful ARC against the clear blue sky. The next three parts of your talk are the ARC elements—Awareness, Reframing, and Commitment to Action.

Awareness defines the problem or issue.

You give some brief historical background, and tell stories about how you or others first encountered the difficulty. Mention ways the problem might affect your audience's lives. Trigger their connections with the issue. What exactly is wrong? Why is it important to them? Make sure everyone is on the same page and has a personal connection with the problem.

Reframing describes the new paradigm, and shows how you learned to look at the situation from a whole new angle, as an opportunity for growth or better business.

This is the meat and magic of the talk, where you turn the problem into a possibility. Use logic and personal stories to turn their way of approaching this problem upside down.

Commitment to Action.

What steps can your audience take *now* to get the desired result?

With *Awareness*, you grab their thinking.

With *Reframing*, you turn their thinking around.

With *Commitment to Action*, you catapult their thinking into the future.

At some point, you may choose to move away from this structure—but my advice is to master it before you let it go. Let's look at each of these three ARC elements.

Awareness of the problem

In the Awareness part of your talk, you describe clearly what the problem is *for your audience*, and lay out some of the current barriers to success in this area.

If you were talking about "What Individuals Can Do For the Environment," for instance, you might mention the rape of the rain forests, oil spills, and other global situations—but you might also show how their own health and well-being are affected, and tell some moving stories about individuals in similar circumstances who have suffered.

You might talk about why current political efforts on behalf of the environment have not succeeded: big corporate lobbyists blocking effective legislation, the lack of cooperation among nations, denial and apathy on the part of individuals, and Third World countries willing to "slash and burn" for quick profits, to name a few. You might say how, in the face of these massive problems, and powerful barriers to solutions, most individuals throw up their hands. They don't believe they can do anything worthwhile on behalf of the environment—and so nothing gets done. Nobody fights the bad guys.

If you were talking about how to have more self-esteem, you would make clear exactly what you meant by self-esteem and then describe how elusive it seems for many of us. Even when we do everything right—great relationship, lots of money, a fabulous house or car—lack of self-esteem seems to be a chronic and pervasive problem in our society. You would illustrate your points with personal stories, and stories about others, until everyone recognizes exactly what doesn't work about the present situation.

Some questions to ask yourself in putting together the Awareness part of your talk are:

- What is the problem about which you are passionate?
- Why does the problem exist?
- What efforts have been tried to fix it?
- Why have these efforts failed, or met with only limited success?

Once we know what the problem is, we can begin to turn it around.

Reframing: a new paradigm that solves the problem

Reframing is the magic trick within your talk. You pinpoint the false assumptions that keep people from succeeding in your area of expertise. You bust the old paradigm, or way of thinking, and show through your own experience that *the solution lies in looking at the problem a new way—your way*.

You might share with the audience how you had your back to the wall—and then miraculously, you saw a new way of looking at the situation. When you turned around your thinking and discarded the old assumptions, you started to get results.

You shatter the conventional wisdom on your subject, and bring in the element of surprise. Your listeners think, "Aha!" You take the problem and spin it into an opportunity. This is your punchline, your twist, the alchemy you used to turn disaster into advantage.

Your audience may already suspect that the conventional wisdom is way off the mark. They wouldn't have come to your program if they had the solution. They will follow you anywhere if you systematically challenge what "those who know" are saying and give them new ways to see and solve the problem.

Show them how you came to your new paradigm. Perhaps you had just spearheaded a campaign for environmental legislation — and taken a beating. There you were, depressed at home watching the discouraging results come in on the evening news, and the very next story after the stunning defeat of your campaign was about an elderly lady who collected recyclable items from the park every afternoon and felt utterly fulfilled in making her contribution to the environment. She had never even heard of your proposition, but she talked to the reporter about how good she felt about herself and what she was doing, and her smile lit up the screen.

Maybe you realized that for you, the answer was moving your environmental campaign into your home, and onto a smaller scale where *you* were in charge of whether you won or lost. You set up your own recycling program, educated yourself and your kids about product pollution, started "buying green," and did everything you could around the house to support the environment. You started feeling terrific about your efforts and realized that if everybody did the same thing, the environment would be helped exponentially. Not only that, but everyone would feel more effective, happier, and more in control of their results.

The paradigm shift is from thinking about the environment politically to thinking about it personally, from thinking globally to thinking locally.

In the area of self-esteem, perhaps you experienced a crashing depression when you got everything you thought would make you happy and give you high self-esteem—and then realized that you still didn't like yourself very much. That crash was the incentive to explore what *did* give you self-esteem and make you happy, and you discovered that self-esteem comes from within, not from the external things by which society tends to define it. You explored several good ways to nurture self-esteem from within, and found that they worked. Again, you approached the problem from a whole new angle, and applied a new paradigm.

Show through your success and enthusiasm that if your audience gives up the old ideas and concepts about how to handle the problem, they can have the same success.

Once the new paradigm has sunk in, and they've had their epiphany, you can help them make the commitment to action.

Commitment to Action

If you've gotten your audience on the edge of their seats with a great opening, defined the situation clearly, and offered an exciting new way of looking at the situation, they'll be eager to know *what they can do right away*. Make sure you have something to tell them. Bring to your talk a list of specific action steps they can take to solve the problem in their own lives.

You might offer five or ten things they can do around their homes to protect the environment, or to nurture self-esteem from within. These are the tools they can use right away to get unstuck and begin solving the problem. End with the simplest, easiest, most inviting step they can take—or ask if *they* want to share any steps they've committed to taking right away.

Finally, wrap up your talk with an inspirational quote, or perhaps a closing piece from your opening story, or by taking a minute to tell them what it has been like for you to spend this time with them. Tell them your hopes for them, and invite them to contact you if there is anything you can do to support them.

Just as your opening is really a "closing"—to close them on listening to you—your closing is an opening to their relationship with your solutions *and a lifetime relationship with you.*

Putting it all together

Now it's time to sit down to structure your talk. You've been making this case for years, and living your message. To bring home your point, you have at your disposal hundreds of analogies, metaphors, anecdotes, facts, observations, and quotes—more than you could ever use!

But at any given moment, sitting in front of a blank piece of paper, it may be hard to remember any of them. Or you may remember *all* of them, and have no idea which to use and which to toss.

Here is a method I use to let the talk emerge naturally, organically, and at its own pace. Choose three walls of your office, or get three huge pieces of posterboard. Or start three special computer files. Designate one wall, posterboard, or file as PART 1: AWARENESS. Designate another as PART 2: REFRAMING, and a third as PART 3: COMMITMENT TO ACTION.

Next, get stacks of sticky notes, large and small. Let your ideas, stories, and thoughts rise naturally out of your mind, in no particular order. Whenever something occurs to you that you might want to include in your talk, jot it down on a sticky note, and stick it up on the appropriate wall or posterboard, or type itinto the appropriate computer file.

Is it part of defining the basic problem? Is it part of the paradigm shift? Is it part of a program of action? Stick it there and then let it go. You might just write down a few words to jog your memory. Daydream, brainstorm, remember, and reflect. Over a period of hours, days, a week, you can literally empty your life into your talk! It's a natural way of organizing and letting your talk emerge easily out of your consciousness.

Next, take each part (wall, posterboard, or file) and make a mini-talk out of it. Start each part with a "hello story" that illustrates the point you are about to make. Don't begin with "Okay, let's define the problem." Rather, open the body of your talk with a brief story that *lends itself* to a definition of the problem. At the end of Part 1, *tell them* that you have defined the problem.

Open Part 2 with another brief story of dramatic success with a new paradigm, and spell out the meaning of what you have just told them. Then launch into Part 2. End Part 2 with enthusiasm, summarizing the new paradigm, and then after a deliberate hush, tell a story that brings listeners into the realm of taking action.

The "Rapt Attention" talk

In the last chapter, I gave you the opening for my hypothetical talk on "How To Compel Rapt Attention Every Time You Speak." Here is how it fits with the rest of the talk.

The "Rapt Attention" opening

The personal, universal story I used was about speaking on laughter to a V.A. class of women who were caring for their disabled husbands—and realizing that they knew more than I could ever hope to learn about using humor to cope with difficult situations.

The larger application was that any audience is potentially funnier and wiser than any speaker. I expanded on that to say that every audience is a treasure trove of experience and wisdom that no speaker can match—and suggested that the way to tap this treasure is to put a priority on the *relationship* with the audience.

I promised to show them how to bring out the best in every group, and to give them tools for natural rapport and relationship with the audience that compelled rapt attention from the first moment to the last.

After I collected their agreement that this was something they wanted, I moved into the body of the talk—taking on the ARC elements one by one.

"Rapt Attention" Part 1: Awareness

I define the problem by talking about how the relationship between speaker and audience has been traditionally misunderstood,
leading to an epidemic of stage fright in our society. To lead into
that discussion, I open with a question and a personal story about
my own stage fright.

"I became a public speaking coach because I had the world's
worst stage fright. Who here has stage fright?" [I raise my hand to
indicate that's what I'm asking them to do. Most of them raise
their hands.] "And the rest of you are too frightened to raise your
hands?" [Laughter]

"The first talk I ever gave was a disaster." Here I tell the story of
my Bar Mitzvah speech which I related in Chapter 1, in which
everyone roared when I recited the traditional words—"Today I
am a man"—in a squeaky soprano. The story ends with the idea
that radiating "vibrant vulnerability" is the key to build audience
rapport.

Through stories and asking the audience to recall speakers
they've heard, I identify the problem: most speakers work so hard
to project confidence and power that they sacrifice a genuine,
vulnerable relationship with the audience. Or they are so focused
on their content that they forget about connection. I also talk
about how aspiring speakers see this unnatural approach modeled
so often that they assume it is the path to successful speaking and
struggle blindly upstream, without much notion of connection.
People with stage fright are especially at risk here, since the confident, impervious "presence" they think they must assume in front
of a group is so far from what they actually feel.

Finally, after exploring what goes awry in public speaking, I
conclude that the basic problem is the unexamined nature of the
speaker-audience relationship. Then I pause for up to 15 seconds
as we all ponder the problem and its implications.

If this were a 2-hour workshop, I would invite individuals to
share their experience of speaking in public. If it were a half-day
or full-day workshop, I would divide the them into smaller groups
of four to share experiences, then have a few people share with
the entire group.

This is the end of Part 1.

"Rapt Attention" Part 2: Reframing

Part 2 starts with the good news that there is another way, an entirely new paradigm for connecting with an audience.

I illustrate with stories the difference between being dynamic (like some of the great speakers with whom we might compare ourselves: Winston Churchill, Franklin D. Roosevelt, Martin Luther King) and being magnetic, which is something we can all do by being willing to receive the audience's support. I talk about listening, connection, vibrant vulnerability, and the true nature of the speaker-audience relationship.

By the end of Part 2, I have made the point that being real, and being in connection with our audience, lets us communicate in deeper, more effective, and more life-enhancing ways, and that performance anxiety can be transformed into a strength when we give up masking it.

Now that we have defined the problem and reframed it, we can move on to Part 3, Commitment to Action.

"Rapt Attention" Part 3: Commitment to Action

Part 3 gives people action steps to take these insights out into the world.

First, I talk about nurturing Transformational Speaking attitudes in Speaking Circles—and how once they have experienced the immediate and compelling benefits of a Circle, they will have life-long tools for developing instant and natural audience rapport.

At this point, we divide into groups of four and have 15-minute mini-Speaking Circles so that they get a taste of the experience and become inspired to go out and form their own Circles. First, they go around the circle once for each person to receive silent support for 30 seconds. Then each person gets 2 minutes to talk about whatever is on their minds while receiving positive attention from the group.

Depending on how much time is available, a few people may use the whole room as their Speaking Circle, and share their insights or reactions to the concept with everyone. I try to have at least one person with severe stage fright come to the front of the room to demonstrate a "miracle healing."

Then I tell them how to start their own Speaking Circles at home or at work, and provide handouts describing the guidelines. (This information is in Chapter 17.)

Early in my speaking career, I closed my talks with an inspiring story, quote, or poem. But I've discovered that what works better for me is not a neat ending, but a closing that is more like an opening. I take a minute or two just to stand in relationship with those people and see what comes up for me to share from the silence about our time together. This closing isn't usually rollicking or dramatic, but it is heartfelt and in the spirit of what we've just been discussing. By the end of the talk, people understand and appreciate that.

Remember: keep the focus on your listeners

Kahlil Gibran said, "If [a speaker] is indeed wise, he does not bid you enter the house of his wisdom—but rather leads you to the threshold of your own."

The wisest approach to structuring your talk is not to overload it with your own brilliance and wisdom, but to present specific, easy-to-follow steps that listeners can use to get results.

Putting together your talk can be organic and effortless when you follow this simple structure. It leads your audience naturally through each of the steps they have to take in order to understand your message and make it real in their lives. And remember: whatever makes the talk more fun and satisfying for you will probably make it more fun and satisfying for your audience as well.

The next chapter shows you how to take the most important step you can take toward becoming an effective, inspiring, successful Transformational Speaker, at ease communicating in any arena. It is the secret to everything in this book. ◎

Chapter 17

 ## Your Speaking Circle

The best way to become a Transformational Speaker is to practice, and the best place to practice is in a Speaking Circle.

This chapter is about how to create your own Speaking Circle for friends, family, or business associates in your own home or office. Non-speakers can become fine speakers overnight, just by shifting their attitudes about what the ingredients of good speaking are, and what works in relating to an audience.

How It works

First, let's paint a picture of what a new Circle looks like. We'll talk later about your role as the facilitator (if that's a role you choose), how to keep the Circle safe, and how to handle your own and others' feedback. For now, we'll just look at the "what happens" part of the Circle.

I once asked an extremely successful professional speaker and Speaking Circle veteran what he felt was the most important thing about starting a new Circle. He told me, "Stick with the format, and keep it simple. Whether you think these things are good ideas, or you think you have a better way to do it—do it this way anyway. The whole well of creativity and safety come out of this specific format."

The format described in Chapter 3 has each person taking 3 minutes in front of the group to "check in," then 5 minutes in the next round to speak about anything they want, with feedback.

That is the standard for Speaking Circles. Use it when you have a regular group of people committed to the process, and you have access to a video camera. When you are first starting out, however, I suggest the following modified format.

Weaving the Circle

Begin with a group of four to eight people who want to compel rapt attention every time they speak. They must be willing to support one another, and agree to follow precise guidelines during the session. These Standards of Support are listed later in this chapter. I suggest you read them aloud before you begin.

Arrange the chairs in a circle. The first time around, each person gets 1 minute of silent support and attention. (The volunteer facilitator acts as the timekeeper, and says, "Thank you" at the end of each person's turn.) This person does not speak, but takes in the positive regard and silent appreciation of the group. He or she practices receiving support in silence, and maintaining soft eye connection with one person, then another and another. It's very important that there is no conversation at this point, even between people's turns.

Next, go around the circle again—this time for 2 minutes each. The person presenting takes in the attention and support, free either to speak or not. Although there should never be a formal topic, many people are moved to talk about a current life issue they are facing, a significant incident in their lives, how they are feeling about work or family, how they spent the morning, or what it's like to be the center of attention.

When it is your turn to be the center of attention, receive the support silently for at least a few seconds before speaking. You do not have to speak at all. Your priority is to receive and feel the support for being yourself. Speak only when the spirit moves you.

If you do speak, speak directly to one listener. Pause to "watch" your words sink in. Keep eye contact with individuals in the group, one at a time, rather than scanning the audience. Notice a tendency to avert your eyes or turn inward to figure out what to say next. Gently let that tendency go. Take in the support. Stay with people. Be willing to hang out in the unknown. Stop trying to "hold it together" or be clever.

Let what you say come from your relationship with the group in the moment, not from memory or ideas you brought with you. Allow silences, and let yourself be surprised by what comes up. When you don't know what to say, stay with one person in the silence. There's no rush, and speaking is not the priority. The priority is to receive the support of the person with whom you are connecting. Ideally, you are connecting with someone or other in the audience 100% of the time.

"Dare to be boring" rather than chatter to cover anxiety. Remember that you are completely safe to feel the fear or the elation, the expansiveness or the shyness. The group has absolute patience and supports you completely no matter what you are feeling or saying.

When you are sitting in the Circle watching other people, you may be tempted to think about what you're going to say when it's your turn. Let go of these thoughts. It's hard to give the speaker your complete attention and support when you're thinking about what you're going to say. Also, you'll miss the experience of letting just the right words come to you out of your relationship with the group when it's your turn. Allow what you say to bubble up, rather than planning it.

Five minutes of bliss

By the time each person has had two turns (1 minute in silence and 2 minutes either speaking or not speaking) following these guidelines, there will be a feeling of deep listening in the room. It is almost a sense of grace, or what some people call "ritual space." The group has become a community, and willingly remains quiet even between speakers.

Now each person takes 5 minutes to follow the thread of a feeling, thought, or idea. He or she may tell a story, discuss a challenge or stress, an obstacle, a joy, a sorrow, whatever emerges in this precious atmosphere of support. Again, remember the option to remain silent. The person speaking also has the option of standing in front of the group, or remaining seated.

As always, when it is your turn, take in the silent support before you start. Notice people, catch up with yourself. Explore something perhaps for the first time. Something you haven't figured out. Find the answer as you speak, to get the "aha" in front of the room, or not. This is how we learn to "think on one's feet."

You might tell a story from your life that is still "charged," and see if any new insights emerge. Or talk about your day. Maybe you're facing a challenge or obstacle. See if some guidance comes out of the support. Some people use this time to sing or explore movement. The form doesn't matter; it's all about *connecting*.

The facilitator signals by raising his or her finger when 30 seconds are left. The speaker finishes within that approximate time, and takes the applause into his or her heart. If you have resistance to taking in the applause, notice your tendency to cut it off. Then try to open up to it a bit. Practice taking it in, and this support will be reflected in other areas of your life and work.

After the speaker is finished, the facilitator asks the person to report briefly on his or her experience with the question, "How was that for you?" The speaker shares briefly how it felt to be in front of the room speaking in that way, then the facilitator invites comments from the group. People give brief, positive feedback. What did you like about the speaker? What positive feelings and values came through? *It is absolutely crucial that no one gives advice, "good ideas" for improvement, or comments on the content. We don't talk about the ideas, opinions, or story that people shared.* Only give your personal feelings about how it felt to be with that person as he or she stood in front of the room.

As the Speaking Circle progresses and the room becomes increasingly "safer," people's sharing becomes more vulnerable. Hearts and souls open as people connect with and support one another. Laughter and tears frequently show up.

This all happens only to the extent that we are able to give up the urge to be clever, to entertain others, control the situation, "make something happen," or engage in cross-talk, problem-solving, or advice-giving. Participants are learning to speak and to listen at a deeper level—as individuals and as a group.

The next level

As the group develops purpose and continuity, and plans a regular meeting schedule (every week or every other week is recommended), consider videotaping. You might also consider a microphone and amplifier, as well as moving from a circle to theater seating facing a small stage or riser—although you can start without any of these things.

Videotape adds a new level of magic, as speakers see how good they really are. After an occasional initial negative reaction ("Look at my hair!!" "I'm so fat!!"), people are amazed at how much better they look on tape than they felt when they were standing in front of the room. Watch your first tape at least three times to get beyond those critical voices. Listen to the positive feedback. Start to see the same beauty in yourself that others see, and that you see in them.

The active ingredients of total support and positive attention are addictive. As you become more effective as a speaker and realize you are speaking from the inside out, begin to relish your time in front of the room. Start to feel the joy and satisfaction of your leadership role as you reach the hearts, minds, and souls of audiences with deep emotional impact, natural humor, and the charisma that comes from receiving and connecting with your audience.

Holding the space:
your job as facilitator

As the facilitator, you model support, listening, and positive attention for the group. You are the person to whom people can
look for complete acceptance and encouragement. Make the Circle a "listening meditation" for yourself. Says Circle facilitator
Cherie Diamond:

> A fringe benefit of being a facilitator is that my listen-
> ing skills have improved. I am now a "peaceful listener."
> Through the practice and discipline of listening to speakers
> who expect conscious honest feedback after their talk, I have
> learned to listen unconditionally without my having to sort,
> classify, analyze, project, predict, censor, approve of, or dis-
> approve any of it. I can relax, knowing that the best feed-
> back will surface on its own, like cream on milk. Hearts
> open as the speaker emerges and freely expands into the
> space created by the peaceful listener.

In the end, the safety and power of the Speaking Circle comes
out of our clear intention for safety and power. By treating it as
sacred—the space, each person, and the process—then that's what
it becomes. We see the essence of each individual, and watch each
person blossom. We can make it safe even for the shyest people
by talking about the beauty of vulnerability, how we are all afraid.
By respecting people, wherever they are, they respect themselves
more. By our optimism, they notice their unique strengths. Expect them to succeed and they do!

Even if someone is slow to receive support, or they find it difficult to let go of artificial style or "schtick," just be patient and
supportive. Make the space even safer by encouraging them to be
exactly where they are. Sooner or later they will come around, if
they stick around.

Also an important piece is that each person has equal time in
front of the room. Some may feel that what they have to say is so
valuable that they can keep talking well beyond the 30-second
signal. If this happens, remind them privately that the content of

the talk or getting their problem aired is not the point; it's the connection that matters.

Holding people to their time limit is important because we are free to listen to and support a person completely *if we know when they're going to stop*. Outside of Circles, people often talk for much longer than most others can tolerate. If we know they will stop in 5 minutes, we more easily put aside our inattention or judgments.

Suppose someone completely loses his or her connection with the group, or runs amok in some other way. It's never ideal to intervene when someone is in front of the room, because you're saying implicitly something is wrong. But sometimes I give a cue to "breathe" by connecting with them silently from where I'm running the videotape while taking a deep breath myself.

More rarely, I'll say "No rush" if someone is speeding forward and has lost the group. Or I'll just gesture with palms down to indicate, "Stay here with us. Stick with us." Sometimes I'll even say those things out loud. This is a very delicate issue and calls for good judgment when to intervene and when to let people continue in their struggle. Usually it's best not to intervene—but if your gut tells to, do it quietly and gently, and be willing to back off if they resist you.

The "art" of being real can't be taught. Each person has to discover their own way. Support and trust them as they are, and just wait for the magic!

The safe container:
quality control

Jane Bell, a teacher and leader of spiritual journeys, facilitates Circles in her home. She says, "What works is creating a container of safety so that people know that whatever they do up there, they will receive love and attention. Most people have never had that in their lives. It's a profound experience to know that the group's honest intention is to give you that.

"When you really realize that, you can begin to unpeel the mask. But if you think someone may take a shot at you or not pay attention, you may shut down. I believe Speaking Circles create a place for natural evolution, where natural human souls can emerge."

As a facilitator, you create "the safe container" of a Speaking Circle. You guarantee that people will receive unconditional support, and that the room will be safe.

The secret is to set the tone in the beginning. In a gentle and conversational way, talk to people from your heart about the safety of the room. Begin by reading and getting agreement on these Standards of Support, the official guidelines to which each Circle member needs to agree. You may type and distribute them, and discuss them before you begin.

Find out if group members are willing to agree to these guidelines. If they are not, they are discouraged from attending. The safety must be absolute. Each participant has to make safety and support their number one priority.

Standards of Support

A Speaking Circle is as effective as the room is safe. For optimal safety and best results for all, we agree to maintain the following Standards of Support.

Confidentiality.

- We do not take content of talks outside of the Speaking Circle, unless we have specific permission.

While a person is presenting, we as audience members, to the best of our ability:

- Maintain soft, positive focus on the face of the speaker
- Remain quiet except for laughter if it comes up naturally
- Do not take notes or engage in any other distracting behavior
- Do not respond out loud, even if asked a question by the speaker.

When giving feedback, we do:

- Keep it brief (no more than 30 seconds) and clear
- Frame it absolutely in the positive
- Talk about *our* own feelings.

When giving feedback, we do not:

- Discuss content of the talk
- Talk about the speaker's life
- Evaluate or compare this talk with previous talks they've given
- Analyze, coach, or advise
- Turn attention to ourselves.

When receiving feedback, we:

- Just receive it into our heart the best we can
- Do not make comments to the people giving feedback, beyond "thank you."

During breaks and after Circle:

- We are sensitive about initiating conversations with others on the content of their talks. This includes good ideas, prying questions, and unsolicited advice.

If you are unwilling or unable to maintain any of these Standards of Support, please bring it to the attention of the Speaking Circle facilitator.

Troubleshooting

No matter how much agreement you get about the safety of the room, sensitive issues arise.

How about a person who tells jokes or makes comments that may be racist, sexist, or otherwise offensive to others in the Circle? What if someone wants to take off their clothes? Isn't the rule that you can do anything? How about the sensibilities of other group members?

We need to trust ourselves to deal with these situations intuitively. The answers may vary from group to group, night to night, and from facilitator to facilitator. Trust your gut, decide what you want in your living room. I have taken people aside after the Circle and asked them not to repeat certain behavior: telling jokes that have a victim, or reflecting contempt for people in or out of the group, for example.

Generally, people who are not supportive and sensitive to others aren't attracted to Speaking Circles. Or they come once. The format itself filters them out, though some occasionally slip through. Use your own judgment about where to draw the line, and when.

The line between what is okay and what is not okay is "fat and furry," like the caterpillars we all are as we turn into butterflies. The facilitator needs to be good-natured, yet fiercely protective of the safe space. Here are some things that tend to get in the way:

- *People who approach others at the break to talk about the content of their talk.*

  Sometimes this is okay, but people have to be careful. They should always ask the other person if it's all right to respond about content.

- *Giving advice.*

  Again, this often happens at the break, when people relax and forget about the rules. It doesn't matter if people have to be respectful when you're in front of the room, if you know they can ambush you in line to use the bathroom at the break. Participants can brainstorm ideas by mutual consent at some point *outside the Circle space* if they wish.

When trouble crops up threatening the safety of the space, a way must be found to redirect it without unnecessary discomfort to the person who has gone off course. Often, they just need to be reminded of the guidelines.

Group energy often leads people toward safety. When people tell the truth about their lives, a common interest in maintaining a safe space is generated. If someone is on the edge, the group energy will pull him or her in a supportive direction even if nothing is said.

Cherie Diamond discusses some of the quandaries and rewards a facilitator encounters.

> How can we be firm about support standards while still maintaining an atmosphere of safety? How do we handle our own irritations when people are late or wait until the last minute to tell you their tape isn't cued up, the equipment breaks down in the middle of a talk, participants express anger or exhibit behaviors designed to attract negative attention? How do we stay on the rim and not fall into the vortex?
>
> Declaring that your game is unconditional positive regard means that sooner or later the opposition will show up. This is a rehearsal for real life, a chance to maintain the integrity of our commitments and exercise the emotional muscles needed for "becoming medicine," for being part of the solution.

Feedback: yours and theirs

When a participant finishes a talk, ask them, "How was that for you?" They may reply briefly, for example:

- "Well, I felt a little nervous at first, but then I calmed down."
- "It felt *great!*"
- "It felt *awful!*"

You give two or three sentences of succinct, positive feedback to set the tone for other people's feedback. Your guidelines are the same as for the audience: only positive feedback, no advice or analysis, no comparison or suggestions for improvements, no discussion of content, or good ideas. Acknowledge what you liked about them today. What you say that is truthful and based on your own emotional reaction will be "right." Trust your instincts.

You might start your feedback by responding to their answer to your question "How was that for you?" For instance, to the three comments above, you might say (if it were true):

- "I could feel it when you relaxed and connected with us. You warmed up the room in a wonderful way."
- "It felt great out here, too! Your enthusiasm came shining through."
- "Thanks for being willing to show that you feel awful and not hide it. That's the kind of courage that works here over a period of time."

After your feedback, it's time for others to give the speaker feedback. Let the speaker call on people. Without expectation that everyone give feedback, people usually enjoy giving positive feedback once they get the hang of it. The bottom line is that it makes us feel good to say nice things to and about others.

It's very rare for someone to give feedback that is negative, but sometimes people can't resist giving the speaker advice—about their speaking, their life, or their topic. It may take many forms:

- "That could be a professional talk, especially if you'd…"
- "I went through a time like that a few years ago, and I think it would be helpful for you to know that…"

- "I just want to say, and I know we're not supposed to talk about content, but I once had a car that was a lemon, too, and what I did was..."

The other "slippery" kind of feedback is comparison. It sounds positive, but suggests that the speaker has overcome something bad that audience members were too kind to mention before:

- "That's the best talk you've ever done."
- "You really opened *up* today; I finally see who you really are!"
- "I'm not embarrassed for you any more."

The key is to stay focused on how it felt emotionally to be sitting in the audience when that person was in front of the room. Another good guideline for feedback: *Don't reflect a belief that you know any more about speaking, or about life, than the speaker does. If your feedback is coming from "professional expertise" or the experience of years, don't say it.*

As with speakers who may do offensive things in front of the room, the delicate part is knowing how to maintain the safety of the space without making the person who's giving the inappropriate feedback wrong. One way is to do preventive maintenance by reading the Standards for Support before you begin. Explain that feedback can be very sensitive and subtle. You might even go over some of the pitfalls we've just discussed, using examples. Let them know that your job is to keep the room safe, and that you'd like their support. Remember that feedback is an art form, and people need some time to practice and get the hang of it.

When in doubt, stick with the guidelines.

The world of the Circle

Each time a Circle meets, a new community is woven. The evening's themes flow into one another, and people become connected in new ways. The next time that Circle meets, they begin from a place of deeper connection. As the Circle continues to meet, the connecting increasingly deepens.

In cities where there are many Circles, such as the San Francisco Bay Area, people often attend Circles that are not their "regular" groups—and they find that there is a larger community of people whom they may not have met, but who share the Speaking Circle experience and values. People from all over the country are starting to meet one another and recognize an even larger community.

As the Speaking Circle community expands and becomes stronger, we shine our light on other people with whom we have contact. Whenever a new Circle forms, the larger circle expands and our community grows stronger, wider, and deeper. Each one of us becomes more committed to supporting one another, and to receiving support from others.

I am committed to making this work available to anyone who wants it. If I can support you in any way, or if you would like to order my video on "How to Conduct a Speaking Circle," please use the order form at the back of the book, or contact me:

> Lee Glickstein
> Center for Transformational Speaking
> 450 Taraval Street, #218
> San Francisco, CA 94116
> 1-800-610-0169.

I picture each one of you in front of a Circle of support, and send you my love. ◎

Order Form

Please print!

Please send

Be Heard Now! How to Compel Rapt Attention Every Time You Speak **and/or** *How to Conduct Your Own Speaking Circle* (videotape) **to:**

Name _____

Address _____

City _____ State _____ ZIP _____

_____ book(s) at $16.00 each $ _____
_____ videotape(s) at $19.00 each   _____

Add 7.25% sales tax for products
shipped to California addresses
($1.16 per book, $1.38 per videotape)   _____

Shipping and handling
    First class:
    $3.00 for the first book or videotape   _____
    $0.50 for each additional book or video   _____
    OR
    Book rate (allow 3 weeks):
    $1.50 for the first book or videotape   _____
    $0.50 for each additional book or video   _____

Total enclosed $ _____

Mail your check payable to:
Leeway Press
450 Taraval Street, #218
San Francisco, CA 94116

Call us at (800) 610-0169 to find out about quantity discounts.